The Turnaround: Parenting Tips For Improving Your Child's Academic Success

The Turnaround: Parenting Tips For Improving Your Child's Academic Success

HOW TO MAKE YOUR CHILD SMARTER, LEARNING-READY AND NONVIOLENT

Deborah L. Kelly, MEd, CPE

ISBN-13: 9781500852122
ISBN-10: 1500852120
Library of Congress Control Number: 2014914738
CreateSpace Independent Publishing Platform
North Charleston, South Carolina

This book is dedicated to my children and husband,
who have loved me through my growth process.

This book is also dedicated to all parents who want to develop a child
who is smarter, learning-ready, and nonviolent.

Table of Contents

Poems:

About the Author

Deborah L. Kelly, MEd, a certified parenting educator, has been married to Ron for thirty-nine years and has two children, April and Michael; three stepchildren, Michele, Ron, and Robin; a son-in-law, Jim; five grandchildren, Chiquita, Kelly, Nathan, Rahnee, and Christopher; two grandsons-in-law, Allyn and Kevin; and three great-grandchildren, Kayla, Kylie, and Alexie.

Deborah has taught pedagogical skills to teachers, facilitated parenting workshops, taught various business subjects at the high-school level, tutored elementary-school students in English and math, taught English in a summer program, facilitated employment-readiness workshops for unemployed men, taught and secured employment for severely emotionally disturbed students, written summer articles for parents regarding providing summer activities for their children to prevent learning stagnation, and established a business as a part-time entrepreneur. Deborah has received various awards, including the Frances B. Bowers Award (1976), Temple University, and Who's Who Among America's Teachers (2005). She was inducted into the Pi Omega Pi Honor Society (undergraduate level) and Omicron Tau Theta Honor Society (graduate level).

Deborah believes in the following tenets:

- **Treat your children as if they are already what you want them to be, and through your efforts, they will become what they ought to be.**
- **Your inner thoughts become your self-fulfilling prophecy.**
- **How you perceive the future shapes your present behavior.**
- **What you experienced in your past can be your point of return.**
- **Don't let your past failures define you.**
- **You will win if you never surrender.**
- **Being jealous is a way of blaming someone else for your feelings of inadequacy.**
- **Liking yourself is half the battle.**
- **God is always good.**

Acknowledgments

I want to thank God for helping me write this book and for bringing me through the tough and rough phases of my life. I want to thank my deceased mother, Elizabeth (Lil) Taylor Bussey Staton Edmead, for her endearing love, her constant support, and for showing me the way. I want to thank my dad, the late Lonnie Staton, Sr., for his love and for showing me life's lessons. I want to thank my stepdad, Howard (Ed) Edward Edmead, for his love and support. I want to thank my daughter, April and my son, Michael, for without your love, encouragement, and support this book would not have been possible. I want to thank my step-daughter, Michele and her husband, Jim, for their love and for their devoted parenting to Chiquita, Kelly and Nathan. I want to thank my step-son, Ronnie, for his love, kindness, and for his devotion to his son, Christopher. I want to thank my step-daughter, Robin, for her love and for her devotion to her daughter, Rahnee. I want to thank my step-granddaughters, Chiquita and Kelly and their husbands, Allyn and Kevin, for their love, kindness, and for their devotion to their children, Kayla, Kylie, and Alexie. I want to thank my step-grandson, Nathan, for his love. I want to thank my brother, Lonnie Staton, Jr. (author of *How to Rent Rooms in America, How I Made Millions Renting Rooms and So Can You*) and his wife, Elaine, for their love and encouragement. I want to thank my sisters, Gloria, Sandy, Bisa, and Nadirah, for loving me. Finally and not least, I want to thank my husband, Ron, for his love, devotion, and for supporting me throughout this project. I want to thank all other family members and friends who encouraged me during the process of writing this book. It is sincerely appreciated.

I want to thank Dr. Adele F. Schrag, former professor at Temple University, for her teaching, guidance, knowledge, and belief in me. I want to thank Mr. Charles Wilson, former principal of McKinley Elementary School, for giving me an opportunity to develop professional parenting skills. I want to thank Mrs. Diane Wagenhals, MEd, CFLE at Parenting Resource and Education Network (PREN); Ms. Ann Martin, Pan-African Studies Community Education Program (PASCEP), Temple University; Minister Chike Akua, Imani Enterprises, SuccessQuest/Speaker's BootCamp; and Dr. Darlene Adams for sharing their knowledge with me.

I want to thank Barbara Way Washington (author of *My Amazing Journey of Faith!*), Toni Saunders, and Nadirah Ali for their confidence and encouragement in me.

Thank you all for letting me belong to your lives.

A Note from the Author

t is my hope that, by reading this book, you will have more enjoyable interactions with your child and develop a child who will become more intelligent, learning ready, and non-violent. And, during your child's lifetime, he or she will become lovable, capable, cooperative, smart people with empathy and love for himself or herself and others.

After you use the parent-and-child engagements and interactions mentioned in my *Tips*, your child will more likely be self-actualized. **Self-actualization means to be able to care about others, to take risks, to be optimistic about the future, to love herself or himself and others, to acquire and maintain healthy relationships, to be self-fulfilled, and to be better able to cope with life's disappointments.**

This is done through proactive parenting and through planning discussed in this book. By being proactive, you control and facilitate positive outcomes for your child and family as well as eliminate conflicts among family members and others. Don't be dismayed by delayed gratification. The result of your efforts may not be totally seen until your child reaches adulthood. However, positive results should eventually be seen. I am excited about your potential results!

This educational enhancement system is not a homeschooling system to be substituted for formal education. It is meant to be applied and used at home in cooperation with formal education.

Introduction

As a former public high-school teacher, I have seen many unmotivated students who were functioning beneath the ability with which they were born. These were students who did not feel smart or intelligent, capable, or ready to learn. They were willing to sabotage their learning to avoid letting anyone know that they didn't feel smart enough. Consequently, they developed behavior problems. The negative behaviors that students develop are because of self-fulfilling prophecies and a failure mind-set, which are self internalized through outside messages. These outside messages have communicated that they are not smart, that they are not welcome, that they are not good enough, that they are not lovable, etc., leading to a self-fulfilling prophecy. Self-fulfilling prophecies and failure mind-sets are difficult to change because motivation comes from within. Positive motivation is built in a person from a young age by preparation, by building confidence, and by instilling a success-oriented mind-set. Thoughts come before behavior.

The sad truth is every year, over 1.2 million students drop out of high school in the United States of America. About 25 percent of high-school freshmen fail to graduate on time. Almost two thousand high schools across the United States graduate less than 60 percent of their students. Statistics show that in Philadelphia, Pennsylvania, over half of all students drop out of high school. The student truancy rate has risen. Fighting among students is rising. In the United States, only seven out of ten ninth graders will get high-school diplomas, and high-school dropouts commit about 75 percent of crimes. They potentially earn $200,000 less than high-school graduates over their lifetimes and almost $1 million less than college graduates. One of every three Black males in their twenties will experience the judicial system. There has been a 500 percent increase in the prison population in the last thirty years to approximately 2.3 million. Most of the incarcerated have no high-school diploma, cannot read on grade level, and may be deficient in cognitive development.

In an effort to reduce truancy and dropout rates while also increasing test scores, some schools have reduced class sizes, reduced teacher-student ratios, shown subject relevancy with work opportunities, provided better and more interesting teachers, provided project-based teaching, decreased teacher lecturing to no more than fifteen minutes, complied with the No Child Left Behind Act, formed homogenous groupings, provided individualized instruction, and instructed teachers to show "love," just to name a few possible solutions. The students' results have changed little because the solutions are reparative and remedial. They don't fix the problem of students who start school unprepared and unmotivated. I believe the solution to these problems lies within the home environment—a simple lifestyle change that prepares a child for learning and success.

A purposeful, intentional lifestyle is essential when developing children who are smarter, learning ready, and nonviolent, and it has nothing to do with your paycheck. Many successful and smart people have come from low-income households. Increasing your child's IQ (intelligence quotient) and giving him or her the necessary tools for success begins with making small changes on a daily basis.

A better lifestyle is obtained through intention (having purpose behind behavior) and increased knowledge, which results in making better choices and decisions. This book will give you—the parent—the knowledge necessary to create a lifestyle that is conducive to increasing your child's IQ, building his or her self-confidence, and preparing him or her for success.

This book should also help families stay connected with other family members, which is the strongest institution and foundation that exists. The analogy I would make is that the family is as a bunch of grapes connected by the vine. The family is as the vine, and the grapes are as each family member, each of whom is characteristically individual. If the grapes fall from the vine, they whither and begin to decompose, even transforming into raisins.

When children are born, their minds are empty slates. We are born only knowing how to suckle. Children need their minds filled with an abundance of information and knowledge. Filling children's empty slates and broadening their abilities to take in large amounts of knowledge and information are key. The earlier their slates/minds begin to be filled, the greater their intelligence and the higher their proficiency level potential will be. Your goal is to increase mental capacity by effectively helping your child take in, retain, dispense, and use information. You do this by putting in large volumes of information while making the process fun and stopping before a toleration level is achieved. You want to stop before your child is frustrated and turned off. Intelligence is not awakened at a magical age but develops by building on previously learned knowledge and skill over time. Lifelong learning is an outcome.

My belief is substantiated by John Bowlby (1950):

> *Depriving a child of intellectual knowledge and skill building stimulation can stunt intellectual development. The direct studies (of the effects of deprivation) are the most numerous. They make it plain that, when deprived of maternal care, the child's development is almost always retarded—physically, intellectually, and socially—and that symptoms of physical and mental illness may appear. Such evidence is disquieting, but skeptics may question whether the retardation is permanent and whether the symptoms of illness may not be easily overcome. The retrospective and follow-up studies make it clear that such optimism is not always justified and that some children are gravely damaged for life. This is a somber conclusion, which must now be regarded as established.*

If a child has been deprived of mental stimulation by being placed in a room alone, the child will not develop at the same intellectual level and rate as his or her counterparts and will have difficulty catching up (possibly never catching up). There is a window of opportunity (a limited amount of time to acquire skill proficiency) for neurons to attach to behaviors in order to proficiently master tasks by a certain age. The younger the child, the more engrained the knowledge or skill will be. If the window of opportunity is missed, the skill may not be learned to proficiency level.

The ability to learn decreases by the age of five; therefore, filling the empty slate/mind with as much information as possible is essential before a child starts kindergarten. Your child's academic success lies in your hands. You are like a potter on a potter's wheel. The potter can mold a small pot holding a small amount or mold a larger pot holding a larger amount. You, as a parent, are as a potter who can create a pot capable of holding a larger amount of information and knowledge. You have the power to create and expand the learning capacity of your child, allowing him or her to take in and process large amounts of knowledge and information. You can do this by inputting large volumes of information and making the process fun. You have the responsibility to prepare your child to be a problem solver and a capable thinker, as well as a lovable, compassionate, and productive human being. Teach your child to embrace him or herself—mentally and physically. You can do this by interacting with and stimulating your child's mental development. This will help to prevent the fourth-grade failure syndrome, where African American males start to decline in academic success in the fourth grade.

The greatest gift a parent can give his or her child is preparation for maximal learning, total acceptance, and unconditional love regardless of circumstances. We need unconditional love to flourish, to develop positive self-esteem/self-worth, to maintain spontaneity, and to become self-actualized. I will talk more about self-esteem, spontaneity, and self-actualization later. Everyone has a need to be loved, recognized, acknowledged, and respected within the family and the outside environment. If you are intelligent and self-actualized, you obtained the knowledge and acquired the attribute with the help of someone else.

When we listen to stereotypes about the poor people in the United States, it sounds as if there is a huge difference between what the poor and what the rich aspire toward for their children. There really isn't. The poor and rich want the same things for their children—academic, emotional, and financial success. Both groups want their children to be capable, lovable, and productive. Then what is the difference between them? The true differences between the two are lifestyle, knowledge, and educational opportunities. The poor do not want less for their children; many just lack the knowledge to make better choices and decisions for their children.

Your child can be smart, capable, and lovable if you do simple things on a regular basis. It's up to you, because you hold this power according to what you do on a regular basis. These simple things are provided for you in my *Tips*.

Upon entering kindergarten, a five-year-old child should know:

- their mother's and father's full names;
- their home address and phone numbers;

- their birth date;
- the entire alphabet with sound recognition;
- colors;
- geometric shapes;
- body parts;
- how to count to one hundred;
- the names of days of week/months of the year;
- weather elements;
- seasons of the year;
- fine motor skills (tying shoes, buttoning coats and shirts);
- position words ("left," "right," "up," "down," etc.); and
- the difference between "good touch" and "bad touch."

This may seem like a lot of information; however, you have five years, and it can be easily accomplished through play and regular interaction. It is easier for a teacher to build upon information and knowledge if all students start with the same knowledge level. Imagine the challenge in a classroom when students start with different knowledge levels. Those students who know less will probably be challenged less by teachers.

There are two educational resource Internet sites I will recommend to be used with your child in cooperation with my *Tips*. They are starfall.com and ABCMouse.com. There are other sites; go on the Internet and search "educational sites for parents."

Parents usually parent the way they were parented unless a conscious decision is made to parent differently. Awareness for a need for change takes place first. You can't change what you don't recognize needs to be changed. You may have to make that decision without feeling guilty or disloyal to family tradition. If you want different results, you must put different behaviors in place. The definition of insanity is doing the same thing and expecting different results. If you want different results—for children to be smarter, more cooperative, less violent—you have to use different behaviors. Parents should identify and set expectations based on desired success outcomes and plan for ways to achieve these goals. Doing this before having children is even better. Many parents will begin reading parenting resource books before their child is born. (See Reading Guide, Multicultural Parenting Resources on page 151.)

If you have low expectations of yourself as a parent, get off your back, onto your stomach, and crawl toward becoming a better parent. Don't wait until your feelings change to put different behavior into place; just do it. It will be a delayed gratification, and you may not see all the desired results for years to come. However, the end result is the most important. Think in terms of what legacy you want to leave behind. What you put into place today will be your legacy for future generations to emulate.

> *Take the first step in faith. You don't have to see*
> *the whole staircase, just take the first step.*
> —Rev. Dr. Martin Luther King, Jr.

Note: **Your use of electronic technology (cell phones, Internet, iPods, iPads, Kindle) can interfere with and take time and quality away from positive parent-child**

interactions. When you are with your child, no more (with few exceptions) than ten minutes of phone conversations and computer time should take place. You will still be reading; however, it should be everything your child is reading.

There can be two perspectives on parenting effectiveness— your perspective and your child's perspective. One day I was at the home of a friend. Her mother came to visit, and when the question of child rearing came up, she said, "I know everything about raising kids. I could write a book." When she left, my friend said, "That book would have two sentences: Shut the f*** up, and I'll kick your a**." That is not very effective when raising children, especially from the child's perspective. Don't let your child feel less appreciative of your parenting efforts. This is an example of a parent who thought she'd done a good job raising and disciplining her children, but she did very little to build self-esteem and self-confidence.

Parents, think about the effect and consequences of what you say to your children before speaking. I know this is sometimes difficult. However, the benefit outweighs the effort of scrutinizing your words. By using my suggestions and being a united front with your spouse or partner, you will be a proactive parent first and leave the relationship with your child open for eventual friendship later. Your child needs an effective parent, not a friend. Also, you don't want to regret not instilling enough knowledge or skill development before your child exits high school. After that time, it may be too late for him or her to welcome your advice.

Rod Paige, former Secretary of the US Department of Education, indicated that there are five things that contribute to academic success: how much a child reads after school (the more, the better), how much homework is done after school (sufficient amount for reinforcement of day's lesson), amount of TV watched (less is better), the child's school attendance (the more, the better), and parents' school involvement.

Parents, visualize your success, and enjoy the great interactions you will have with your child through my *Tips*. Remember, time goes by so fast, and time and quality moments cannot be retrieved.

When engaging the following *Tips*, always remember:

- **Start from the least difficult and progress to the most difficult (i.e., start with number recognition and counting, then move to addition, and then to subtraction, multiplication, division, etc.; division should not be taught before subtraction or multiplication).**
- **Learning should be built on previously learned knowledge or skill (i.e., teach the alphabet through phonetics—the sounds of letters—and then assemble words).**
- **Make the learning process fun (i.e., use music, dance, games, rhymes, flash cards, etc.).**
- **Stop your routine when your child is ready by noticing when he or she is distracted or**

becomes inattentive or fidgety. Stopping will help your child develop a desire to continue the learning process during the next session.

- Don't carry frustrations from the previous day to the next day's activities. Start with a fresh, positive attitude and outlook each day.

- Provide examples to compare what they know with what they don't know (i.e., use examples from your child's experiences).

- Provide love and patience during the entire process. Showing anger or frustration will paralyze the process.

- Make a spiritual connection with your child. This is done by being in tune with and receptive to your child's needs and by showing total acceptance and unconditional love through eye contact and connecting with the inner essence of your child.

- Separate your child's behavior from your child. Your child may behave unacceptably; however, your child is always acceptable. Make that distinction.

- Treat your child as if he or she has already achieved what is expected of them, and through your efforts, he or she will consequently become what they ought to be.

- Visualize your success; believe that your child can accomplish your goals. See the desirable outcome in your mind's eye.

The following Tips should be implemented from as young an age as possible, except for Tip Number Twenty-Six, which deals with financial knowledge.

Now, let's get started developing smart, learning-ready, capable, and lovable children!

TIP NUMBER ONE

Pick Up Your Child When They Cry

When your child is an infant, pick him or her up every time he or she cries. Crying is a form of communication that allows babies to indicate that they are hungry, wet, uncomfortable, or distressed. When parents learn the difference of each cry, they can respond accordingly. When babies receive the expected response, they will learn to trust their caregivers. They will learn that their verbal communication is effective and they will have the incentive to continue to develop their verbal and nonverbal communication skills. Additionally, the more you pick up your baby and satisfy his or her needs, the less your baby will eventually cry and the more independent he or she will become at an earlier age. A crying, fussing baby will not efficiently learn. If you pick up your baby when crying during the day, he/she may be more cooperative at bed time. You may use a different strategy for developing a routine at bed time.

Picking up and cuddling your child will also enable you to bond with them, developing a lifelong connected and trusting relationship. This leads to an increase in your child's confidence, self-security, and spirit of cooperation. When you cooperate with your child by acknowledging his or her needs, it helps your child to develop cooperation with you, creating a self-actualized person—an individual who loves and respects him or herself, who is outward centered (caring about other people as well as him or herself), who takes risks, who is optimistic about the future, who loves him or herself and others, who is fearless, who feels worthy of success, and who will acquire and maintain healthy relationships.

Rene Spitz did an experiment and reported that children raised without emotional warmth were deficient physically and emotionally (1945).

Some will disagree with this philosophy, but think about this: when you are hungry, stressed, or uncomfortable, and your immediate need is not met, do you feel cooperative, pleasant, or learning ready? Your child will have a difficult time learning and focusing if her or his needs are not met.

There will be times when you will have to remind your child to communicate verbally with words instead of crying. Just say, "Use your words." Do not say, "Stop crying" or "Stop whining." The latter could appear critical and could affect self-esteem development. When your child speaks, let him or her know you are intently listening.

Cradle and rock your baby in your arms with as much skin-to-skin contact as possible, as well as singing and talking in low, loving tones. The more you talk to your child, the more intelligence is built. Plus, it will enable you to bond with your child. This is a basic need. Do not miss this most important opportunity to bond and form a lasting union and trust with your child. If you miss this window of opportunity, you may miss the best opportunity to bond. Not bonding with your child could create a void in his or her life, which could manifest in inappropriate behavior later. As human beings, we have a need to bond with significant others. If your child does not bond with you, he or she could bond with other people or elements, which could be unsavory gangs, cults, material possessions, sex, promiscuity, work, etc. I also believe parents who have developed and cultivated a loving, healthy bond with their children are less likely to be abused by their children. Bonding with your children will also decrease the likelihood that they will develop drug and alcohol addictions and depression in the future.

Drugs anesthetize the emotional pain of not feeling seen, heard, or valued. We learn to value ourselves when others have valued us. Self-sabotage, low self-esteem, low self-confidence, risky behaviors, and violent tendencies are all symptoms of not valuing ourselves. Even when we think healing has taken place, we can revert back to old behaviors when under stress or not feeling loved. Be aware that old behaviors can resurface when we don't want them to. *Remember, your past can be your point of return; live every day with purpose and intention.*

A feeling of cooperation, confidence, and self-security is a result of having our needs met. When you have confidence, you feel secure and competent, as though you can accomplish anything. It frees you to concentrate on the outside world instead of being self-centered and only concerned with your unmet needs. It frees you from self-consciousness, enabling more spontaneity—acting from internal impulses instead of acting based on what others think.

Meeting your child's needs is his or her first experience with learning cooperation. Children will more likely do what is asked of them and follow family rules and guidelines if their initial needs are met.

Your purpose should be to prepare and treat your child the way he or she should expect the world to treat them. If abuse is given, your child will accept and tolerate abuse from others. When children's needs are satisfied, they are more likely to see the world as a cooperative place and more willing to cooperate with others. They will be free to satisfy others' needs.

There is a big difference between meeting a child's needs and spoiling him or her. Meeting your child's needs outweighs the risk of spoiling him or her. Spoiling is treating your child in a way that causes the child to expect unrealistic returns for the effort given. When children are consistently being given things and having nothing required of them, it causes them to demand or expect too much.

> Circle of Moms members feel strong that you can't spoil a baby by holding or comforting him or her too much. In fact, they believe the opposite: that meeting an infant's need to be held and fed in a predictable fashion actually helps your baby feel more secure and will build a lasting relationship of trust between mom and child. "Human infants are born incredibly vulnerable," says Lisa M. "They're also biologically programmed to need near-constant contact with their

mothers. Basically, a baby feels out of sorts and wrong when not being carried. A dry diaper and a full belly just can't cut it," Jennifer L. says, adding that "A baby needs to be held, it isn't even that they just want to be, they actually need it. Human contact is essential for proper brain, cognitive, and emotional development." What's more, many of Circle of Moms members feel that responding to your baby actually fosters independence. "I held my son all the time, I still pick him up when he is crying," says Nikki M. about her 13-month-old son. "I don't believe you can spoil a baby, a baby needs their mommy to comfort and soothe them. Studies have shown babies who are not left to cry are the ones who are the most independent later on, because they feel safe and secure. My son is the most independent little boy out there." Many Circle of Moms members also agree that cuddling and holding a baby fall into the same category of basic needs as feeding and changing dirty diapers. As Angie E. explains, "The need to be held and cuddled… is as much a need as any of the other things. It's how they build attachments and learn that they are safe. Remember the baby has just spent nine months living inside of you, hearing your heart beat all day long and being warm and cozy. How scary must it be for them to suddenly be put in a big crib all alone with no heartbeat to listen to, no warm cuddly place where they can hear your voice?" So next time someone suggests that a baby is purposefully turning on the waterworks to yank your chain and be spoiled, don't pay attention, suggest Brandy K. "If your baby is having some separation anxiety and is being extra-needy, wanting to be held all the time, the quickest way to get him through it is to be there for his every cry. Knowing that you are there for him all the time, whenever needed, will build his confidence and support him in becoming an independent person. Mothers are supposed to be nurturing, and babies need to be held and comforted." ("Why You Can't Spoil a Baby" by Mary Beth Sammons, June 10, 2011, http://moms.popsugar.com/Why-You-Cant-Spoil-Baby-273310011)

Before your child turns two, you will not spoil him or her by giving him or her lots of love and attention; you are just giving your child what is needed to successfully progress to the next emotional level based on Maslow's Hierarchy of Needs. Think in terms of giving your child what she or he needs to sustain her or him for life. Your child's unmet needs may produce behavior that gets in the way of you knowing his or her true temperament and disposition. Negative behavior stems from unmet needs. Our unmet needs and wounded spirits are difficult to heal. They manifest and spiral into inappropriate behaviors, remaining as scabs and never really healing without therapy. Having unmet needs interferes with appropriate emotional development and makes it less likely for a person to reach self-actualization.

We teach our children how to love by providing food, clothing, and shelter, and by establishing trust and safety. It is worth providing because tenderness and feeling loved stay with us for our lifetimes. If you do not teach your child how to love, your child will be more susceptible to violence and fighting.

Behavioral psychologist Abraham Harold **Maslow's Hierarchy of Needs Theory** posits that to reach self-actualization, a sequential hierarchy of needs should be satisfied. **Self-actualization** enables a person to be outward centered—to care about other people as well as him or herself, to take risks, to be optimistic about the future, to love him or herself and others, to be fearless, to feel worthy of good things in life, and to acquire and maintain healthy relationships. When one set of basic needs is satisfied, a whole new set of needs surfaces to be satisfied. If a set of basic needs is not satisfied, a person can be emotionally stunted at that level and may never progress to the next level of emotional development toward self-actualization.

To paraphrase Maslow, to become **self-actualized**, there are **five sets of needs** that should be satisfied. The first basic need to be satisfied is **providing food, clothing, and shelter** for your infant—to be fed when hungry, to wear warm and comfortable clothing, and to be in a safe living environment (first set). If these needs are not provided, a person will not feel safe and secure and will not likely establish a feeling of **trust and safety** (second set). Who would trust a caregiver if he or she is hungry, cold, or afraid? If a person cannot feel trust and safety, he or she will not be able to **love** (third set) and establish healthy loving relationships without suspicion of motive. If a person does not feel love, she or he may not develop a healthy **self-esteem** (fourth set), which can translate into not feeling worthy and capable. Children blame themselves when love is not given, and they feel undeserving of love, which effects self-esteem. If a person has not developed healthy self-esteem, he or she will never be truly **self-actualized** (fifth level) with the attributes listed above. It is said that only a small percentage of our population reaches self-actualization. We wonder why our children are not more successful!

As a parent, consider it may be more difficult to satisfy someone else's needs when your needs had not been met as a child and also have not been met as a concerned mother or father. This will make it more difficult to meet the needs of someone else. However, it is worth not repeating this pattern. Remember to be attuned to your needs and lovingly ask family members for what you need.

Diane Wagenhals, author of *PREN's Parents Reference Guide: 25 Essential Tools and Tips You Need for Emotionally Healthy Parenting* (2005), said:

> Need deficits can easily spiral. You may have come into adulthood with significant needs unmet and feel sadness or pain sometimes when dealing with your child. These feelings may be a product of your unresolved childhood experiences. Consider that a toddler is predictably very needy physically, emotionally and socially almost all of the time. His mother has extra needs herself during this time: she needs lots of insight into her child's behavior, recognition for the important job she is doing, a good night's rest, ways to fulfill all of her in-home and outside-home responsibilities, and some time alone. Under so much stress, she may have trouble fulfilling her role as caregiver and may not have energy left to appreciate other familial relationships. The stress created from these feelings of apparent neglect can intensify and negatively impact everyone in the family. She needs and deserves support in adequately meeting her needs. Mothers and fathers both

deserve to have needs met, and their relationship also has its own needs as well!

Remember that children learn most effectively when they are stress-free. Make sure your child is comfortable and feeling safe to facilitate learning.

TIP NUMBER TWO
Hug and Kiss Your Child

Hug and kiss your child every day. Tell your child you love him or her and how special he or she is to you. When you put your child to bed, when you wake your child up, when you see your child off to school, and when your child comes home from school, greet him or her with a hug and kiss. Find something good and encouraging to say to your child at least once a day. Whatever you exalt and acknowledge is what your child will try to repeat and achieve.

Focus on behaviors and less on appearance. Say, "I liked the way you used your manners when you…" or "I liked the way you helped out with…" or "You did a great job with…" or "Your studying paid off when you got a good grade in…" or "Your hard work paid off with…" or "I admire you when you…" However, be careful with using phrases like, "You're the most beautiful," "You're the most talented," or "You're the smartest." These statements could appear to be unrealistic and untrue, and your child could also develop negative attributes, such as self-centeredness, conceit, or arrogance. You want to show and give messages of support, respect, lovability, and capability, such as, "You can do it," "You can accomplish it if you work hard." We develop healthier self-esteem and are more successful when we are acknowledged for our accomplishments over our looks and appearance.

> *Only a man's character is the real criterion of worth.*
> —Eleanor Roosevelt

When your child enters a room, your eyes should light up, and he or she should always be acknowledged. Take advantage of every opportunity to develop in your child positive self-esteem and self-concept (how your child perceives others and how he or she thinks others see him or her). This may be the only opportunity in your child's life when he or she will feel special, which is necessary in developing positive self-worth and overall sound emotional health. Children gather and internalize messages about themselves from how they are treated and what is said to them about themselves on a regular basis. They believe you and take it literally when you criticize them. If you say they are stupid, lazy, or no good, they will believe you and act accordingly—which becomes a self-fulfilling prophecy. Your message will become the message they send to themselves. The messages we send ourselves about ourselves become our self fulfilling prophecy. It can be difficult to change these negative behaviors later. We look at ourselves through the eyes of others. Only use positive labeling or titles for your child (e.g., Champ, Ace, Prince, Princess, Lady, Precious, Angel).

Do not focus on your child's mistakes; focus on your child's attributes and qualities. This will help with building high self-esteem and self-concept, which leads to self-confidence—the feeling of not needing assistance. State what behaviors you would like to see instead of what behaviors you do not like. For example, say, "When you enter, hold the door with your hand so it does not slam" instead of saying, "Stop slamming the door!"

Never miss an opportunity to be kind and to show your child love and empathy. A benefit of providing a warm, friendly, and loving environment is that your child will be more likely to adopt your values and customs and become warm, friendly, and loving people. Note: Children will go through various stages and will outgrow negative behaviors, such as the "terrible twos." However, children will never outgrow the feeling of not feeling loved.

According to Rudolf Dreikurs, Adlerian psychiatrist, when children don't feel loved or when a child's goals are not satisfied, a child's mistaken approach to satisfy his or her goals can be taken. In paraphrasing Dreikurs' **Four Mistaken Goals of Misbehavior Theory**, he said there is a mistaken or negative approach used by children whose goals are not satisfied—**Undue Attention Seeking, Rebellion, Revenge, and Avoidance.**

Undue Attention Seeking is when children don't get attention when exhibiting positive behavior, so they seek attention through negative behavior. Children need attention. Children will get attention from negative behavior or from positive behavior because behavior is needs based.

Rebellion is another type of misbehavior that happens when a child doesn't have any control over his or her environment—no power, no independence, and no ability to make decisions.

Revenge is a mistaken approach when a child feels unprotected, abused, and unable to make a valuable contribution.

Avoidance is a mistaken approach children take when they cannot withdraw in quiet time and center in a positive way. Children need down time to regroup.

Dreikurs says children need **attention, power, protection, and withdrawal time**. If these goals are not satisfied, children will use the mistaken/negative approaches to get what they need.

Do not favor one child over another. Treat all children with the same amount of love and attention. The favored child will be resented and disliked by his or her other siblings. I heard Oprah Winfrey say that her best friend, Gayle King's mother made all of her children feel favored and made to feel special—a gift to all of her children.

To paraphrase Alfred Adler, a behavioral psychologist, he believed that in order to thrive as human beings, it was important to understand his **Surviving-Thriving Cycle/ Three Goals of Belonging, Learning, and Contributing**. Adler believed we need a loving base in which to **belong** and stay connected with significant others with whom we feel safe. We therefore are motivated to **learn**, which leads to the satisfaction of **contributing** to our community and to the world. This, in turn, enhances a feeling of belonging and a secure base, which leads to an attempt at new learning, which leads to positive contributions. A positive self-esteem will surface, and your child's behavior will be healthy, positive, and capable of cultivating healthy relationships. Making a valuable contribution is what builds self-worth.

When you cease to make a contribution, you begin to die.
—Eleanor Roosevelt

Developing routines and rituals in which the family takes part together will help develop a base of belonging in your child. Routines and rituals include eating meals together at least once a day and family activities and games, including Go to the Head of the Class, Candy Land, War, Uno, Outburst, Inklings, Sequence, chess, checkers, Chinese checkers, backgammon, Monopoly, Scattergories, Catch Phrase, Jenga, Scrabble, Guesstures, Taboo, Ping-Pong, billiards, reading, puzzles, and family outings to movies (explain and discuss what is viewed and articulate your values), miniature golf, bowling, skiing, roller-skating, and ice-skating, just to name a few.

Also, find opportunities to have your child participate, volunteer, intern, or give back. Ask your child's school counselor, your municipality, political headquarters, city or state representative, community groups, and local businesses about opportunities in which your child can partake. Opportunities should be within the child's age and ability range.

Building a solid base with your child through staying connected is basic and is most important. Keep in mind that daycare and nursery schools may provide a safe environment for
your child; however, in most cases, they do not provide necessary and important nurturing—neither do you want the
daycare or nursery to provide the ultimate base of belonging.
Refer to "Child Care Selection Criteria" in this book.

We once had a family dog named Thor. When he came to us
at approximately twelve weeks old, the agreement was that my
two children would take full responsibility for feeding, walking,
and training him. When I began to pet him and talk to him,
Thor began to lose his feeling of unfamiliarity. He loved me
most of all, and I never fed him; I just provided him with love,
and he reciprocated the love. Everyone in the family knew how
Thor felt about me. Love is the strongest emotion with human
beings and even with some types of animals.

To further my conviction, psychologist Harry Harlow con-
cluded from a series of experiments in 1958 with infant rhesus
monkeys and a set of "surrogate mothers" that attachments (an
emotional bond to another person) and the need for affection
were deeper than the need for food and the need to explore.

TIP NUMBER THREE

Discipline Techniques
That Motivate

Obtain and use a discipline technique that motivates your child to want to make correct choices and decisions without damaging their self-esteem and self-confidence. The purpose of discipline is to get someone else to choose different behaviors without wounding or incapacitating their core belief system (set of beliefs about ourselves and our relationship to the world). Don't feel bad when you have to discipline your child; children want rules and boundaries. Never forget you are teaching a child how to operate within guidelines and boundaries which will be expected of them in society. Show your child that all behaviors have consequences. Clearly articulate house rules and boundaries. It is effective to post the rules where your child can visibly see them.

Consistency in delivering immediate consequences is necessary. Don't wait until the following day. Always immediately address inappropriate behavior. Parents should model the behaviors they want from their children. It is easier for a child to duplicate the behaviors of people with whom they live.

Using embarrassing or belittling tactics, which make a child feel bad about who he or she is, does not work. It will only make your child focus on his or her undeveloped characteristics, make your child feel self-conscious, make your child develop low self-esteem, and hamper him or her from positively moving forward with his or her emotional growth. Your words of criticism can remain with your child longer than your encouraging words. You will have more problems if your child lacks self-confidence and has low self-esteem. Often, people who feel bad about themselves do bad things. It is a self-fulfilling prophecy.

Never withdraw love as a form of discipline. Your child will need more love and understanding when you discipline him or her. Let your child know that you have unconditional love for them, and nothing he or she does could change that.

Separate your child's negative behavior from the child with phrases like, "You are a good person, but I don't like what you did." Making bad decisions or choices does not make a person bad. Your child must feel that he or she is a *good person* who just made a bad choice or he or she could behave as a *bad person*. Totally eliminate calling your child "bad." *Your inner thoughts become your self-fulfilling prophecy.* The self-fulfilling prophecy could become reality. There is an old saying, "Be careful what you call yourself; you might answer." You don't want to unintentionally produce a bad person.

> *Identity determines activity.*
> —Minister Chike Akua

Let your child know that sometimes good people make bad decisions; however, everyone should be given an opportunity to make things right. Let the child know that he or she can redeem him or herself and make the negative action right by apologizing, by doing additional chores to earn money to make restitution, or by making a plan and following through to restore the situation. All three of these things will help to heal and restore a child's self-concept and self-image. Afterward, acknowledge and give your child credit for rectifying the situation. Start each day new and fresh, and do not carry over what happened from the day before. Identify whether bad behavior is done due to obstinacy (stubbornly resistant) or lack of knowledge of good-choice behaviors. Don't assume that your child knows what the desired behavior is. Always articulate each step of the desired behavior. Also, when a negative activity is taken away, that time spent should be replaced with a positive activity.

Don't always take your child's inappropriate behavior personally. It may not be directed toward you. No person is perfect. Look for possible causes for inappropriate behavior. Is your child experiencing fear, pain, hunger, or emotional hurt? Then you can decide the appropriate remedy or action to be taken. Your plan of action should be based on your child's underlying needs motivation—relational needs, emotional needs, or whatever the outward behavior could be communicating.

Diane Wagenhals's PREN identified an **"Iceberg Analogy,"** where there are three levels of emotional health: the tip of the iceberg above the water, which represents **outward behavior** (behaviors we can see); the second layer just beneath the water, which is larger in size and refers to **emotional health** (self-esteem and perception of self); and the third layer, which is the deepest and largest, and which represents **relational health** (quality of how children were nurtured and relationships with parents and significant others). When trying to change outward behaviors, you must recognize and heal emotional and relational health. Just as a cough is a symptom of germs brewing within the body, the outward behavior is a symptom of germs brewing in underlying levels. When identifying and selecting what discipline strategy you should use, the layer of health should be considered.

> *Every child seeks and desires a self picture as capable and strong, and behavior matches the self-image. A basic rule about human behavior is that negative feelings exist before negative acts. We focus on the act and ignore the feelings causing the act.*
> —Dorothy Corkille Briggs, *Your Child's Self-Esteem*

> *Mind is the Master Power, it moulds and it makes; man is mind, and forever more, he takes the tool of thought and he fashioneth what he wills. He can bring forth a thousand joys or a thousand ills. He thinks in secret and it comes to pass; his environment is nothing but a looking glass.*
> —James Allen, *As A Man Thinketh*

It is imperative that parents motivate their children to want to change from within. This is what will last longer than the fear of getting caught. Change should be seen as a positive goal for their inner needs being met and felt. They should see consequences of good behavior as a payoff. Sometimes children misbehave because they get the consequence they need when they behave inappropriately—such as attention. Give more attention when they behave appropriately.

Some suggestions for dealing with discipline include **"I-Messages," "Logical and Natural Consequences," "When-Then" Statements, and "Either-Or" Statements**. Make sure that with whatever discipline technique or strategy you use, your child's outcome will be the inner motivation of wanting to make good and honest decisions/judgments for him or herself.

"I-Messages" are effective when the parent is directly affected by the child's behavior. They allow the parent to say how he or she feels about the child's behavior without blaming or labeling the child. They create a situation in which the child is more likely to hear what the parent is saying because it is expressed in a nonthreatening way. They clearly convey to the child the parent's feelings about the child's behavior, putting the emphasis on the parent and his or her feelings, not on the child and the child's character. The child does not feel personally attacked. When delivered clearly and firmly, I-Messages often influence the child to change his or her behavior. Keep in mind that I-Messages are less effective when the child has not bonded with the parent and is therefore less likely to care about the parent's feelings.

When a child gives a negative response, talks back to the parent, or displays other disrespectful behavior to a parent, I-Messages can be given.

There are four steps in giving **I-Messages**:

1. **Say specifically how you have been affected by the situation**. This statement could begin with "I feel hurt," "I feel disrespected," "I feel unloved," "I feel put down," "I feel my authority has been usurped," etc.

2. **Name the specific behavior or situation**. This part of the message is a description of the present behavior or issue and involves no judgment. "When you suck your teeth or roll your eyes..." "When you ignore me..." "When you don't do what I ask of you..."

3. **State how the situation or behavior interferes with your purpose or how the behavior is counterproductive to cohesive family relations**. "Because, if I permit you to disrespect me now, then you will feel it is all right to always disrespect me." "I am given the responsibility of guiding you in the right direction. If you do not listen to me, then you will prevent me from performing my role in your life." "Because family members should care about each other." "Because when you disrespect me I will not respect your needs or wants."

4. **State the desired behavior.** "A productive way to get what you want is to..." "I want you to..." Or even "I would like you to..."

For example: "I feel disrespected when you roll your eyes and suck your teeth when I speak with you. In a well-run household, someone has to be the authority figure—a person in charge. That is my role, and I take that role seriously. Therefore, in showing respect for my authority, you should show compliance by not sucking your teeth or rolling your eyes."

Another example can be: "I feel you've been unfair to me when you leave the kitchen a mess because the kitchen is used by all family members. Someone else will have to clean the kitchen before being able to use it. No one wants to work in a messy and smelly kitchen. A family unit works most effectively when all family members contribute to the upkeep of the home. Therefore, I would like you to clean up and wash the dishes after use." Being in an unclean environment is another way of saying this is all you deserve.

Michael H. Popkin, PhD, Active Parenting, Inc., suggests that parents can use giving consequences as valuable teaching tools. **"Choice + Consequences = Responsibility."**

"Children learn responsibility when they are first given the option of choosing how to behave. Once they have made a choice about how to behave, it is important for them to experience the consequences of that choice. When they experience the consequences of misbehavior, the lessons they learn are more powerful than any lecture or arbitrary punishment." Teach your child that all behaviors have consequences—good or bad.

Giving a child choices and letting him or her feel the consequences of his or her choices and decisions is a better lesson than a parent's lecture or punishment. I also feel when a child takes part in the decision-making process, he or she is more cooperative with following through to a positive end.

> *We have to give our children, especially Black boys, something to lose. Children make foolish choices when they have nothing to lose.*
> —Dr. Jawanza Kunjufu

Logical Consequences are the results parents deliberately choose to show children what logically happens when they violate family rules, values, or social requirements. These are intended to show children how to behave responsibly, and they are administered in a firm and friendly manner without anger or hostility. It is different from punishment, which is an arbitrary retaliation for misbehavior that's intended to impose the parent's will over the child that is too often delivered in an atmosphere of anger and resentment.

Examples of using logical consequences are: When Danny comes home too late for supper, he must heat up leftovers alone and clean up his own dishes. When Susan does not get up when her mother calls her in the morning, she must get dressed in the car while being driven to school. If your child takes something that does not belong to him or her, the consequence should be to take the child back to the location and return the item or the value of the item with a statement of repentance. If a child disrespects his or her teacher or another adult, the consequence should be to have your child apologize or make restitution.

Natural Consequences occur when parents allow the child to experience what would naturally happen when incorrect choices are made and which naturally follow (without parents' intervention) from what children choose to do or not to do. When I was a child, after playing outside in the snow, my mother told me to run cool water over my cold hands instead of warm water. I did not listen to her and instead ran warm water over my hands to warm them. Instantly, my hands started throbbing with pain. I then understood the consequences. I never did that again, and it taught me to heed my mother's advice. Note: Never use natural consequences when the consequences could be dire or irreversible; for example, when a child jumps into a pool without being able to swim well or when a child touches a hot stove.

You may step in and save your child from consequences only if the consequences are irreparable, unredeemable, or dangerous. Instead, you may want to explain the consequences or show them a picture of the consequences.

A child will not behave in a way that does not bring gratification. Dr. Popkin believes that when children have choices, it makes them more cooperative and responsible. He feels that, when given the opportunity, children will always make choices and the consequences of those choices will teach them how to make similar choices in the future. He believes if benefits are derived from consequences of misbehavior, then that misbehavior will continue. If no benefits are derived from the consequences of misbehavior, the misbehavior will change. In other words, "Kids don't do what doesn't work." To be effective with using consequences, the consequence should always be related to the misbehavior. An apology, restoration, or restitution should be directly related to the misbehavior.

Either-Or Statements are another way of giving your child choices and making him or her feel empowered within appropriate boundaries. They may be phrased as, "Either you may wear the blue pants or you may wear the green pants today. You decide." Both choices should be desirable choices for parents.

Here are other examples: April sings and babbles loudly while her parents are talking. Positive phrasing would be, "April, either you may play quietly here, or you may go to your room. You decide, dear." The logical consequence of continuing to distract the parents is to give up the pleasure of their company. Poor, ineffective phrasing would be, "April, stop that racket, or else you'll have to go to your room." Another positive example would be: Michael is teasing a puppy. The parent says, "Michael, you can either pet the puppy gently like this"—and demonstrates the proper behavior—"or you can take him back to his box. You decide." The logical consequence of continuing to tease the puppy is to lose the privilege of playing with him. Poor, ineffective phrasing would be, "Michael, stop teasing the puppy, or I'll make you take him back to his box."

When-Then Statements are a way of stating what could logically happen when certain behaviors are demonstrated. They can be phrased like this: "When you put out the garbage, then you may eat breakfast." Other examples of when-then statements would include the following: April is watching TV when she has been asked to make her bed. "April, when you have made your bed, then you may watch TV." The logical consequence of April not making up her bed is losing the privilege of watching TV. Or, perhaps Michael is about to leave for the swimming pool, ignoring his regular Saturday task of cleaning the bathroom. "Michael, when you have finished the bathroom, then you may go swimming." Do not use poorly phrased choices, such as, "Michael, you may not go swimming until you have cleaned the bathroom." If Michael starts for the swimming pool without cleaning the bathroom, the parent can say in a calm, nonthreatening way, "It seems to me that you have decided not to swim today. You may try again tomorrow or next week."

You should provide the choices only one time and then act immediately to put the consequences into place. Do not condition your child to hear your request more than once; you could be setting a pattern and conditioning your child not to respond the first time. Parents should interpret the continued misbehavior as the child's choice. Negative consequences should immediately follow, or the value of the lesson is lost.

Allow your child to try again to select appropriate behavior after experiencing the consequences. Discussing the problem with the child beforehand can be done to help set consequences, therefore making them easier to enforce later. Ask your child what he or she feels the consequences for inappropriate behavior should be. Make sure the consequences you decide upon are logical. Children see the justice of logical consequences, and they usually accept them without resentment. But, if a consequence you decide upon is not related to the child's misbehavior, it will seem arbitrary and punishing. For example, if your child goes to a friend's house without asking, the consequence is that he or she should not be allowed to go to any friends' houses for a designated period of time. The consequence should not be extra cleaning, restriction from a family outing (especially if the child would miss an opportunity to gain a life skill or exposure), or spanking. These consequences do not relate to the behavior.

Diane Wagenhals' Parenting Research and Education Network believes that if parents give too little, such as not enough attention, love, or affirmation and give too much responsibility at a young age, or give too much, such as an unrealistic showering of attention and love and not enough responsibility, the child can develop **destructive entitlement**, which takes the form of low self-worth and invalidation, distrust, and untrustworthiness. She bases this belief on Ivan Boszormenyi-Nagy's **Ethical Dimension Theory**, who was the founder of Contextual Therapy. Individuals with destructive entitlement, without being cognizant, feel there is a bottomless debt that is owed them, which is difficult to fill. These people become only takers, which is frustrating in relationships which should be reciprocal. Self-worth, self-validation, trust, and trustworthiness can be built by turning destructive entitlement into **constructive entitlement** by giving the child credit (e.g., acknowledging his or her triumph over a situation or longevity of suffering) and also by giving the child an opportunity to give back to others. Here are two examples of how you can do this: First, you could say, "I'm sorry," which is a way of giving the child credit for pain he or she has suffered. When you apologize, you are giving credit to the hurt person, which frees him or her to start the healing process. Second, you could say, "Everyone deserves a good parent, and you deserve a good parent. Unfortunately, that is not what you got. I admire the decisions you have made in spite of your situation. You can help other children who did not get good parents by helping them by mentoring through a Big Brother or Big Sister Program."

I believe hoarding is a form of destructive entitlement where there is a bottomless barrel that cannot be filled, even with an excessive amount of things. However, the person continually tries to fill it.

Remember to give positive feedback when your child gives back and involves him or herself in good behaviors. Acknowledge and praise the behaviors you want repeated. Try to eliminate what could be perceived as criticism. Recognize your child's positive characteristics and accomplishments over focusing on his or her negative behaviors and weaknesses. Remember, behavior is need-based, and there is normally a payoff. If the only time we get attention is when we are acting inappropriately, then we will act inappropriately to get attention. Give your child more attention when he or she is acting appropriately. For example, you could say, "I like how you shared with your sister." Or something like, "You were so quiet while I needed you to be." Or even, "I'm so proud of how you held your temper and calmly handled the situation." Make sure you give more love and affirmation than you give constructive feedback.

I was once in the presence of a mother who had a history of not giving her son the attention and contact he wanted and needed. While she watched television, her son threw a ball as hard as he could and hit her in the head. I could see what his motive was. He needed attention from her and was willing to do whatever it took to get it.

> *Poor self-esteem develops from receiving little or no feedback, being repeatedly criticized, receiving physical or mental abuse, feeling invisible, or feeling unloved.*
> —Popov, *The Family Virtues Guide* (1997)

Your goal in disciplining your child is to help him or her develop self-discipline so that positive behavior will continue when you are not around. The result you want is that no matter how many people around your child choose to do wrong, he or she would still choose to do right. Communicate that standing alone is not a lonely place. It is a place of peace and contentment through God. Let them know that he or she with God is a majority.

Say what you mean and mean what you say. When you say no or yes, mean it. Don't ever joke with your child by saying no or yes when you do not mean it. It is confusing and neutralizes the effect of your attempts at discipline. Let your child know that he or she can depend on what you say. Be a model by keeping your word. That is what your child will think the world will expect of him or her.

Never leave your child unsure of what undesirable behavior took place or how that behavior affected others, including you. It's best to explain the desired behavior and why it's the better choice.

Never leave your child mentally or spiritually wounded by your selected discipline choice. How the child perceives the future shapes his or her present behavior. Remember to model the desired behavior you expect of your child—how you handle crisis, interactions with other people, responsibilities, etc.

Early intervention, addressing inappropriate behavior, is necessary for quicker remediation. The later you wait to intervene, the more difficult it might be to change inappropriate behavior. *You will win if you are consistent and never surrender.*

> *Fervor is the weapon of choice of the impotent.*
> —Frantz Fanon

I feel Fanon means that using the sword and punishment is a weapon of the powerless. Using effective discipline techniques, patience, and love gives parents power and motivates children to make better choices.

TIP NUMBER FOUR

Expose Your Child to Different Patterns and Sequences

Expose your child to as many different patterns and sequences as possible to prepare him or her for formal and informal test taking. To practice different sequences in a fun way, you can count with your child by ones, twos, fives, tens, twenties, fifties, hundreds, etc. Practice different patterns by playing matching and rhyming games, and by finding similarities, differences, and opposites. When riding in the car or on the bus or train, while in a restaurant, etc., repeat various patterns by naming or counting different and similar items, as well as articles of color, size, and shape. While at home with your child, in a fun way, you can practice by using similar techniques including singing, clapping, signing, or dancing. Purchase activity books or programs that include the patterns and sequences listed above from discount stores, book stores, drug stores, dollar stores, Internet sites, etc. so that your child will have fun while learning. You are only limited by your imagination—use your creativity and every learning opportunity around you.

Start stimulating your child's mind as early as possible. If your child appears not to be age ready, go back to the last activity your child responded to with enthusiasm, then progress to the next level. Remember, do not wait too long; there is a limited amount of time for neurons to attach to behaviors that lead to proficiency.

The mind is a muscle, and stimulating it makes it operate more proficiently. A beneficial advantage of this is developing successful test-taking skills. With formal education, test taking usually will begin at age five. Testing should be seen as a measurement of skills and knowledge, emotional, and social development. Formal testing tools include IQ tests, state proficiency tests, college proficiency tests, national proficiency tests, etc. These tests are used to determine "homogeneous grouping," which groups children together with others who are like-minded, potential-minded, and academic-minded and determines their qualifications for academic placement and tracking. **Tracking** is when children are placed in remedial or advanced classes after being tested. Once children are placed in a remedial tract, it is difficult to get out. They usually remain behind for their entire school experience in their level of course curriculum and challenges. Remedial placement would not be necessary if all parents prepared their children for the necessary proficiency levels before they started kindergarten. You can do that by using my *Tips*. Note: In some school districts, tracking can be done to your child without first getting parental permission.

Informal testing tools include employment aptitude tests. Preparing your child with test-taking skills will later also give them an edge with employment opportunities.

If necessary, seek out test-taking strategies from the Internet to ease them into and prepare them for test taking.

TIP NUMBER FIVE

Read to Your Child

Read to your child age-appropriate books starting at birth. Some mothers believe that reading to your child while in uterus is effective. The younger the child, the larger the book's pictures and words should be. Make sure your child can view the pictures while you talk in soft, loving tones. Speak slowly and enunciate; repetition is required at first. Later, speed up the pace and eventually have your child read to you. Start with reading for approximately a half hour every day and gradually increase the time depending on your child's desires. Make reading an enjoyable ritual for your child. While reading, ask your child what the story is about, who the main character is, who the villain is, and who the good character is. Ask him or her to predict the outcome of the story and so on.

Reading is one of the foundations of learning. Minds that are exercised by reading perform better with other tasks and on tests. Reading to your child can also improve your child's listening skills, retention skills, and recall skills. Even critics of the structured educational systems say it is better to teach reading early. I have known children who had started reading by age two. Don't let this window of opportunity for skill development close. Children who do not read at their grade level are more likely to develop behavioral problems in class and are more likely to later drop out of school.

I believe teaching phonics is better than teaching word recognition. When letter sounds are taught (phonics), a child can decipher and build words based on the sound of each letter. He or she will be able to decipher and sound out the unrecognized words. I've heard good reports from parents on programs like Hooked on Phonics.

Select books that have positive images and characters who look like your child. It will help to affirm and validate him or her. It is important that your child see characters engaged in activities that you would want him or her to imitate.

Reading a story can be a great way to bond with your child, especially one with a profound message. Whatever activity you do with your child will be special to him/her. Let your child see you reading as a model.

Make sure your child is reading socially—outside of school by the third grade—to acquire healthy, consistent reading patterns. Every day, have your child read something to you. The more they read the better at it they will become.

Ask your child's teacher for a summer reading list and make sure your child reads during his or her inactive times. I suggest that your child reads for at least thirty minutes a day.

Keep in mind the negative effects technology (e.g., video games, headphones, smart phones, tablets) has on the desire to read. The new technology language with abbreviations, signs, and acronyms diminishes the correct knowledge and usage of Standard English. You should provide opportunities for your child to use Standard English and use the correct spelling of words—through fun interactions, activity books and games. Your child's use of technology could also diminish his or her social development. Provide opportunities for your child to interact socially with others on a regular basis. However, the Internet can also be used for benefit. The use of technology can be appropriately used to enhance reading development through e-books and websites. A website with fun activities for children of all ages is www.rif.com.

The following reading suggestions should be most helpful with reading informational and subject books rather than with casual reading, such as novels and more.

Reading Suggestions

Before Reading Strategies:
Before reading a particular selection, I consider my purpose for reading the material.

Before reading, I ask myself questions that I think may be answered by the selection.

Before reading, I consider what I might already know about the topic of the selection.

Before reading, I look at one or more of the following: the title, headings or subheadings, and pictures or charts for clues as to what the selection is about.

During Reading Strategies:

If I do not understand something in a selection, I go back and reread parts of the selection.

While reading, I ask myself questions about the selection and answer them.

While reading, I try to connect what I am reading to what I have already read.

While reading, I try to summarize what I have read as I go along.

While reading, I try to visualize what is being described.

While reading, I use a graphic organizer such as webbing, mapping, or outlining.

While reading, if I don't understand something in a selection, I ask my teacher or other people for help.

While reading, if I don't understand something in a selection, I slow down my reading rate.

After Reading Strategies:

After reading, I reread parts of a selection that I did not understand.

After reading, I think about questions a teacher might ask about a selection.

After reading, I try to summarize the selection in my own words.

After reading, I evaluate what I have read to determine the author's effectiveness.

AUN: 123461-00000326

TIP NUMBER SIX

Talk to Your Child in Sentences

From birth, talk to your child in sentences in soft, loving tones. Avoid baby talk! The younger the child the more engrained the act will become. The more you talk with your child the more intelligent he or she will become.

Talking with your child redirects his or her energy from the physical to the mental. Your child's desire to talk will be advantageous to you when you need him or her to be still in motion. It will be beneficial when your child is in a classroom setting and will be required to mentally channel their energy. I have also seen children use physical aggression when they could not find words to express their frustrations.

Continual dialogues (interactive talking) with your child will help him or her develop more advanced speech patterns and vocabulary. It is just as easy to teach the word "extraordinary" as it is to use and teach the word "good." Use a varied and extensive vocabulary with your child. Take advantage of your time when riding in a car, on public transportation, in a doctor's office, in a restaurant, etc. When you are with your child, talking on the phone should be minimized, if not eliminated. Your focus should be on your child.

Although learning your culture's dialect or language is important, frequently talk with your child using Standard English (i.e., using correct nouns, pronouns, adjectives, verbs, adverbs, and the correct conjugation of verbs, etc.). Also, teaching your child the dominant culture's slang can be useful for communication and comradeship purposes. The benefit of using standard language is that your child will have more proficient and effective communication skills to use with the family, the work environment, and the English-speaking countries of the world.

> *Mastery of language affords remarkable power.*
> —Frantz Fanon

Children who do not read and who are not talked with are likely to be vocabulary deficient when they enter school. Children who are vocabulary deficient do not perform as well in school when in the same class with students who can be thirty million words more proficient. By reading and talking with your child, you can eliminate this disadvantage and disparity.

> *Be skilled in speech so that you will succeed.*
> *The tongue of a man is his sword and effec-*
> *tive speech is stronger than all fighting.*
> —The Husia, sacred wisdom of ancient Egypt

TIP NUMBER SEVEN
Engage While Bathing Your Child

While bathing your child, sing songs, clap, recite nursery rhymes and poetry; touch and say aloud the names of body parts; count aloud by using fingers; and use gentle physical exercises, saying "up" and "down" when moving in the appropriate directions. Note: consult your pediatrician or physician before doing physical exercises.

Filling the mind with healthy information and expanding the capacity to learn is essential. Later, when developing speech, ask your child to repeat or recall words and phrases. This should help in strengthening memorization skills (mnemonics).

Memorization skills (mnemonics) are developed best by using the following:

Repetition—continually repeating verbally, mentally, or physically. A friend of mine, whose daughter was preparing for a law bar examination, repeatedly stated aloud all the projected test answers while she was cleaning. She passed the bar examination the first time.

Association—linking conceptual relationships, such as remembering a date because it is the same as or similar to another familiar date or number. If a number coincides with a family member's birth date, mentally associate and connect one number with the other. A man who could remember a whole auditorium of people's names revealed that he was able to remember each name by associating something he knew with each new person (e.g., a person with a red nose was named McIntosh or a person having the same name as someone else we know who resembles them).

Using the senses—smell, taste, touch, sight, and hearing. Hands-on or tactile learning is effective because the senses reinforce the mental. For example, use touch to teach body parts and use fingers and toes to count up to ten and twenty. You can also teach fractions by cutting an apple into fraction parts.

Other ways to help remember could be using **acronyms** (e.g., MADD [**M**others **A**gainst **D**runk **D**riving]), using **acrostics** (e.g., MADD [**M**ay I dream-**A** day when all-**D**esired hopes will be-**D**eveloped and achieved]), or by putting informational words to rhythm or music. The above example is used for adult clarity; substitute an age appropriate example for your child.

Take advantage of bath time when your child is focusing to instill knowledge using various mnemonic (memory) techniques.

*Memory determines functional-
ity, value, speed, and capability.*
—Chike Akua

TIP NUMBER EIGHT
Engage While Doing Chores

While doing your chores or household responsibilities, tell your child what you are doing. While cooking, say aloud the names of foods and let your child smell the different herbs and spices from your cabinet. Have your child do helper tasks to assist you while you explain. You will be acclimating your child to facilitate in the kitchen, which is considered the heart of the home.

A parent's responsibility is to prepare his or her child to be independent with conducive life skills to thrive. Involve your child with measuring and completing cooking and baking recipes. Teach your child how to prepare family favorites and to prepare breakfast, lunch, dinner, and dessert. Also, teach your child to clean the house, to wash and iron clothes, to repair or hem clothing, and to replace buttons. Make these interactions with your child a fun bonding experience. Your child may not show immediate appreciation for learning these life skills; however, they will thank you later. My daughter and son thanked me when they became adults for making them sit and watch me cook and participate with helping me prepare meals. They are both proficient homemakers with cooking, cleaning, and washing; and thanks to my husband, they both can repair, install, and build things around the house. Males are valuable assets when they can also cook, clean, and wash clothes. Females are valuable assets when they can also repair, install, and build things around the house. If you don't have the expertise, enrolling your child in home economics or carpentry classes at a high school or vocational school night class would be beneficial.

When engaging with your child and delegating or giving chores, keep in mind that you are also teaching your child how to manage his or her time, teaching the ability to start and finish a project, and reinforcing math and reading skills by using recipes with measurements. Your child doing chores is a prerequisite to job experience.

Provide an environment to continuously expand your child's knowledge through real-life experiences in doing every day chores.

TIP NUMBER NINE
Buy Educational Toys

Buy only educational and developmental toys. You want to select toys that teach processes, strategies, and techniques and that are also fun. These toys can be just as fun as long as they are engaging, colorful, and interesting. You can buy interesting books, including dictionaries or thesauruses, activity books, crossword puzzles, flashcards, games, or other fun activities from which your child can learn. Various activity books can be purchased from a dollar store, book store, drug store, etc. Make sure you *do not* buy toys that can be swallowed or cause the child other injuries. Buy age-appropriate toys; the age compatibility is usually stated on the package of the toy. Computer, cell phone, iPhone, and Kindle use should be monitored by you but can be used and enjoyed in an educational way. When assembling new toys from parts, have your child participate in the assembling process. Following the step-by-step directions with your child is an excellent teaching-learning tool.

You can also buy toys with antique value that will appreciate (go up) in price and value over time. A toy may become an antique after fifty years. When buying antique toys, follow this guideline: Don't buy anything that no one else wants. The higher the demand the higher the price usually asked.

The importance of toys that teach processes, strategies, and techniques, is illustrated in the following anecdote. I heard a gentleman at a forum, Haki R. Madhubuti, speak about his childhood. He said that when he was younger, he begged his mother for a beautiful blue airplane. When he finally got the airplane, it became one of his favorite toys. His mother did housework for a family in the suburbs of Detroit. When he visited the home, he wandered into the bedroom of the son, who was his age, and he saw an airplane on the desk that the son had assembled, painted, and flown himself. He began to wonder about all the skills that had been used, learned, and processed during the development and completion of this plane. It later occurred to him that it wasn't just the end product that was most important, but also the process—the skills and knowledge learned that lead to the end product—that is the most important lesson in the learning process.

These process skills in education are called "transfer skills," which can be transferred to other situations, problems, and circumstances when needed. Learning the process to obtain a correct answer is more important than being provided with the correct answer. One of a child's greatest benefits from learning is to gain transfer skills and processes that can be used in other real-life situations. An old Chinese proverb says, "Give a man a fish, and he will eat for a day. Teach a man to fish, and he will eat for a lifetime." This is what parents need to do—teach strategies, techniques, and processes for finding the correct answer as opposed to giving them the correct answer.

It is a benefit to teach the **Decision-Making Process** as opposed to giving a solution:

- Step one: Define the problem.
- Step two: Identify your choices or alternatives.
- Step three: Evaluate the advantages and disadvantages of each choice.
- Step four: Choose.
- Step five: Act on the choice.
- Step six: Review and reflect the outcome of the choice.

If the outcome of the choice you selected is undesirable, go back to Step four, Choose another choice, and repeat Steps five and six.

Eggland, et. al., *Introduction to Business*, Mason, OH: South Western Publishing, 2003.

> *The mere imparting of information is not education. Above all things, the effort must result in making a man think and do for himself.*
> —Dr. Carter G. Woodson, 1933

TIP NUMBER TEN

Engage While in the Supermarket

While in the supermarket, show and say aloud names of fruits, vegetables, and other products. Use foods you will purchase and let your child smell and touch at the same time. As age permits, ask questions such as: "How many apples are in a dozen?" "How many are in half a dozen?" "If one orange costs twenty cents, how much would two cost?" "Three cost?" "Four cost?" "If I have two dollars, how many oranges can I buy?" And so on. Ask your child to calculate, based on his or her allowance, how long it would take to save up to buy a particular item. This is an excellent way to teach mathematical skills, and you are teaching in context—in the environment in which these skills are needed and used. With contextual learning, the skills taught are more likely to be remembered.

Have your child write the grocery list for you. You can gain insight into how well your child is developing writing and spelling skills. Be as creative and challenging as you wish, within your child's ability range. Talk to your child about a grocery budget and how to select grocery items that are economical and healthy and within the grocery budget. Also, discuss item price times volume. Sometimes, instead of manufacturers raising the price per item, they will lower the volume.

> *Learning is doing, and doing is learning.*
> —John Dewey

Teach your child what to look for when buying ripe fruits and vegetables. Fragrance and color of fresh fruit can communicate freshness and ripeness. Select foods that are nutritious, economical, and fresh. Nutritious, fresh food is connected with good physical and mental health. You are what you eat.

Teach supermarket fruits and vegetables labeling prefix codes. Usually a four-digit code starting with a four or a three means traditionally grown with pesticides; a five-digit code starting with a nine means organically grown and not genetically modified; and a five-digit code starting with an eight means genetically modified organism. I believe we have the right to know before purchasing if foods have been genetically modified or engineered. The long-term effects of GMO and such foods have not been determined.

Any retail environment can be used as a learning tool. Take advantage of every opportunity to enlighten your child.

TIP NUMBER ELEVEN
Provide a Space for Creativity

Prepare a supervised space for your child to sit where crayons, coloring books, child's safety scissors, paper, paste, etcetera, can be accessed and used at your child's convenience. A small table and chair in a selected space will allow your child's creativity and imagination to develop and flourish. Creativity is a transfer skill. It is the ability to create various strategies, techniques, and patterns that can be transferred and used in other areas. This is also a way of teaching children how to spend, utilize, and maximize their free time.

Later, also provide a quiet place where your child can prepare and complete their homework.

Minimize and monitor your child's video games, cell phone (including texting), and other technology usage (computer and Internet). Exclusive usage can diminish or delay the development of other skills—interpersonal skills and language development.

Minimize your child's television viewing. The behaviors your child sees can affect values and prompt imitation of unsavory behaviors. Television provides dysfunctional models, behaviors, and perceptions. Low expectations and moral deficiencies are disproportionally placed on ethnic people. The media in general will accentuate the negative stereotypes and deemphasize the positive characteristics of ethnic groups it wants to minimize and make powerless. The **black/white contrast concept** is also repeatedly used by the media when negativity is associated with black and positivity is associated with white (e.g., black day, black cloud, black list, blackmail, black heart, black sheep, black ice, black eye, black hole, black market, black or dark comedy, the dark side, devil's food cake *as opposed to* white collar crime, lighthearted, little white lie, white knight, lily white, pure white, great white, white hat, natural color, fair skin, white noise, angel-food cake). Permanent perceptions can be formed when continual associations are made—one becomes the same as the other. There is a famous experiment where Black children associated a Black doll with being bad, less smart, and unattractive. The effects of associating negative images and characteristics with ourselves could manifest into low self-esteem, poor performance, and negative behaviors. Be careful what messages your child is receiving.

The Black population in America has historically been marginalized by the manipulation of images in the media. Both Whites and Blacks have been conditioned to believe that Whites are superior and Blacks inferior. This has been accomplished by creating negative symbols that define Blacks: poverty, crime, violence, unemployment,

irresponsibility. In fact, Blacks are defined by their problems. This is the tragedy of Blacks in America—that the image is the message and the media is the image.
—Tony Brown, *Black Lies, White Lies: The Truth According To Tony Brown*

My son, when he was approximately three years old, made a verbal revelation to me after watching animation and other child-oriented TV programming about what he had discovered. He said, "Mommy, good guys have blue eyes and bad guys have brown eyes." I had a talk with him about the fallacy of what he had viewed. I immediately talked with him about how a person should be judged and measured by his or her character and not by their appearance. Fortunately, I had already developed verbal communication, bonding, and trust between us that enabled him to let me know what he was thinking. How would it have affected his perception otherwise of his own beautiful brown eyes?

Also, be concerned with the negative portrayal of females in video games and in various forms of media. Female images and characters are too often minimized, marginalized, and over sexualized. Usually, observation of behavior takes place before imitating and acting out behaviors. There is an old saying that what goes in comes out.

Make an effort to curtail your child's television viewing and video-game playing, and have your child spend their valuable creative time building skills and knowledge that they will be able to use throughout their lifetime to enhance their standard of living and quality of life.

TIP NUMBER TWELVE

Take Along Activities

Plan ahead and take along activities for your child to do while waiting in the doctor's office, while traveling in a car, while waiting for meals to be served in a restaurant, and so on—things like crayons and coloring books, reading and activity books, puzzles, pencils, paper, etc. Provide a carry bag of your child's choice, if possible. If your child has a special diet or needs to eat at a certain time, take along the foods that your child will need and want.

Teach your child to spend his or her spare time in a productive way. Where you spend your time most is where you become the best. The brain is a muscle; the more you use it, the better it will perform for you. Have your child use his or her mind in a fun way in his or her spare time.

When I was in high school, I had a business teacher tell a story about how she was selected for a job. She said she was the one who was reading while waiting to be interviewed. The interviewer said he had seen her reading and hired her because she spent her time in a productive way.

When children learn to spend their spare time in a productive way, they are enriching their skills and opening up opportunities for the future.

TIP NUMBER THIRTEEN
Provide Environmental Exposure

Take your child to the park, playground, beach, zoo, circus, fairs, museums, on vacation, or to any fun and safe learning area. Tell your child what he or she is viewing and experiencing in friendly, loving tones. Ask your child what him or her thinks of what he or she is viewing.

When riding in a car, talk with your child on various topics. Here is an opportunity to bond and to provide personal, insightful learning experiences. This is an ideal place because your child is stationary. Impart as much knowledge as possible before your child becomes overly saturated. Turn off all electronics and focus on the dialogue between you and your child.

When walking down a street together, talk to your child about what you and your child are experiencing. Talk about the different architecture, different cars (colors, brands, and models), different types of trees, different flowers, different neighborhoods, different insects, different animals, different types of clouds, different weather patterns, and so forth. Also, give your child lessons on street safety and what to do if a stranger approaches him or her.

The opportune time to begin a dialogue is during your child's formative years. This is an ideal way for the family to stay connected. If this connection is not forged at an early age, children may not have a desire to stay connected later. Being connected with primary relatives encourages the ability to develop healthy relationships with others outside the family—transferable skills. Also, it is an opportunity to teach your child values and how to spend their spare time in positive, safe, and productive ways into adulthood.

> *When you build friendly, warm, accepting relation-*
> *ships with your children, you increase the chances that*
> *they will give your values serious consideration.*
> —Dorothy Corkille Briggs, *Your Child's Self-Esteem*

TIP NUMBER FOURTEEN
Take Your Child to the Public Library

Take your child to the public library to obtain a personal library card to borrow books and to partake in other activities like using technology (computers and the Internet), games, music, reading sessions, animated events, and so forth. Make sure your child is reading books of his or her choice and grade level by the time your child finishes first grade.

Also, seek out and take advantage of other free activities in your community. This is another way for your child to spend their spare time in a productive way, as well as expanding their knowledge base.

Have your child write down his or her expectations for the day before starting. At the end of the experience, discuss how, when, where, and why the expectations were accomplished; and, if not accomplished, examine and identify why.

TIP NUMBER FIFTEEN

Eat Meals Together

Eat dinner or another meal together every day as a family and discuss the day's activities and events (individual, family, local, state, national, international, etc.). Use events, comparisons, examples, and parables to support your viewpoints and ethical beliefs. Ask family members the best and worst thing that happened to them that day. Ask them what happened to them that made them proud. Ask what new fact, theory, or principle they learned. Ask what made them afraid and what made them happy. Ask each family member to share what they are thankful for. Also, share with your child your own successes, mistakes, and positive milestones. Having a "no cell phone and no television" rule during meals together is not unreasonable.

Eating meals with the family reduces the possibility of drug use and delinquency by children. Staying connected as a family with mealtime rituals and wholesome and fun activities, is a drug and alcohol deterrent. Psychologists say that expressing emotions can also lessen suicidal tendencies.

I believe drug use fills voids in lives. Drugs and alcohol relieve the feelings of self-inadequacies, low self-esteem, loneliness (disconnection from the people we love), and other pain. Everyone has a need to be heard, seen, and validated—to be treated as if we matter in the lives of others. The dinner table can be a good atmosphere to validate your children. Children will think they are important when parents give them quality and quantity time.

Children in families that eat dinner together most nights each week are significantly less likely to use illegal drugs, smoke, or abuse alcohol.
—Lois M. Collins, "Family Dinnertime a Powerful Drug, Tobacco, Alcohol Deterrent"

"Parental engagement fostered around the dinner table is one of the most potent tools to help parents raise healthy, drug-free children," says Joseph A. Califano Jr., founder and chairman of the National Center of Addiction and Substance Abuse at Columbia University, in a statement that accompanied the CASA Columbia report. It is said that compared to teens who have frequent dinners (defined as five to seven times a week) with family, those who have dinner with family fewer than three times a week are almost four times more likely to smoke and nearly twice as likely to use alcohol. They are also two and half times more likely to use marijuana and four times as likely to say they expect to try drugs in the future. "This year's study again demonstrates that the magic that happens at family dinners isn't the food on the table, but the conversations and family engagement around the table," Califano argues. "When asked about the best part of family dinners, the most frequent answer from teens is the sharing, talking and interacting with family members; the second-most-frequent answer is sitting down or being together." Dinner time is also a time for strengthening relationships with siblings, the report said.

Jennifer LaRue Huget notes that with busy schedules, it's sometimes hard to get everyone together at dinner time. "The report suggests that it's the act of eating together, not the specific time of day, that matters," she said. "So eating breakfast together five or more times per week should work as well as getting together at dinner time." And here's a bonus finding: teens who eat dinner with their families five or more times a week are one and a half times as likely to report having a good relationship with their moms and twice as likely to report good relationships with their dads and siblings. And to the list of benefits of together mealtime, the project adds better grades, resilience and self-esteem, as well as less teen pregnancy, eating disorders, and depression. The project is a collaboration between several Harvard University researchers and fifteen families (Collins 2011).

> *I've learned that people will forget what you said, people will forget what you did, but people will never forget how you made them feel.*
> —Dr. Maya Angelou

Eating a meal together is also a great opportunity to teach and model social graces, such as saying "please," "thank you," and "you're welcome" when appropriate. Your child will repeat the terms you use. Learning social graces will be a benefit for your child when interacting with others outside the home. Do not be afraid to share family values with your child, even if your child feels they are outdated. Share values on how men should treat women, including not using profanity around women and children, pulling out a chair for a woman when she is being seated, walking nearest the curb and opening doors for women, helping women with their coats, and so on. Teach your child to show respect to older people, men to remove hats inside and at the dinner table, and that a person entering the room greets the people already in the room.

Passing your values along to family is part of keeping your family legacy alive. When you provide a loving, warm, and friendly atmosphere for your children, they will be more cooperative in adopting your values.

Eating meals together is also a good way to teach structure, time regimentation, and sharing concepts. It is an opportunity to teach family, cultural, and ethic history. Eating together also enables the teaching of negotiation, loyalty, teamwork, empathy, and so forth.

When I was in college, I did a paper on time regimentation. I learned that if a person does not take part in doing an activity at the same time every day, time consciousness is less likely to develop. Being on time is taught indirectly at a young age by acquiring these behavioral patterns. It may be more difficult to acquire time consciousness at a later age.

Teach your child to have silent gratitude—to be grateful for the things he or she has in their life and to be able to give credit to himself or herself by showing humble appreciation without conceit and cockiness. Your child should show appreciation for the material possessions parents have provided for him or her, and he or she should be appreciative of his or her physical appearance. Beauty is in the eye of the beholder, and parents should encourage their child to see herself or himself as physically attractive.

Eating together is also an opportunity to teach the concept of sharing through action and context. A family of four has four pieces of meat. Each family member will receive one piece each. It can even be rationalized that parents each get one and a half pieces and both of the children get half a piece because of their size. The concept of family sharing and fairness is important. If you are fair with children, they will learn to be fair with you and others outside of the home.

During large family gatherings, you can prepare a children's table for ages twelve and under. It can also serve as a rite of passage at age thirteen to change from the children's table to the adult table. Parents should acknowledge children when they transition from the children's table to the adult table. If you like, create or find a formal rites of passage ceremony. Ceremonies are always effective and have an impact for a lifetime.

While listening to the radio a while ago, I heard that a father—the late E. Steven Collins, host and executive of Radio One—asked each one of his best male friends to prepare a statement for his thirteen year old son on what they thought a man should know, be, or do. He prepared a venue for his son where they all ate and shared their ideas and advice.

Keep in mind that the family is the emotional nourishment and sustenance of a person. As long as the grapes are connected to the vine, they stay more vibrant and alive. The grapes that fall off the vine will wither and disintegrate.

TIP NUMBER SIXTEEN

Feed Your Child
Wholesome Foods

Feed your child fresh wholesome foods (such as fruits, vegetables, whole grains) from the five food groups. Remember that a healthy body leads to a healthy mind. The brain needs nutrients to grow and function to its fullest capacity.

Puree food in the blender/food processor, and feed that to your baby instead of prepared, jarred baby food from the supermarket. Use broccoli, sweet potatoes, string beans, apples, pears, bananas, etc. When you do this, your child will become acclimated to whole foods and will enjoy and desire them. His or her body will crave what you acclimate them to at an early age. If you start them with processed baby food, they will crave food filled with artificial content. Processed foods have a higher content of sugar, salt, and fat, including the risk of hydrogenated fat content. Artificial coloring, artificial flavoring, and preservatives may also be added to processed foods.

I am an advocate of **breastfeeding**. Many benefits are derived. During the breastfeeding period (which could be up to two years), natural antibodies are transferred from mother to child to help prevent illnesses and build the child's immune system. Mothers will produce in their milk the nutrients needed by their child at each stage of their child's early development. Additionally, breastfeeding is an excellent way to bond with your child. A sense of belonging is satisfied through this bonding experience. Note: If your child does not bond with you, he or she will find another with whom to bond, which could be unsavory. Both of the children I raised went from breast to cup with little effort.

Consult a pediatrician as you decide when and what whole foods and vitamins should be introduced to your child from infancy. Serve cut-up fruits and vegetables for snacks at the age when children begin to eat whole foods. Prepare fresh foods, such as apples, pears, peeled grapes, carrots, and celery with peanut butter or cream cheese. Unfortunately, so-called health bars can be as addictive as any other sugary product.

I have talked with people who say they do not like vegetables. I asked them if their parents fed them fresh vegetables when they were infants. It's amazing that almost all of them say their parents did not make them eat vegetables when they were young. Is there a link between what they were fed from infancy and what they like today? I believe there is. However, you can learn to eat fresh and whole foods at any age—the earlier the better. The longer you wait to introduce fresh vegetables and fresh fruits to your child, the more resistance you may get. There also could be a link between what mother's ate while pregnant and what their child desires after birth.

When my children were very young, I let them eat an occasional ice pop. After eating the ice pops, both children would immediately act in an uncontrollable way. Their behavior was significantly different. I believe it was the artificial coloring and flavoring that contributed to their changed behavior. I started making my own ice pops by using fresh fruit juices. My children loved them, and homemade pops satisfied the same need for them.

Eating fresh foods can also help prevent illnesses caused by nutrient deficiencies. Nutritionally starved brains do not learn as effectively. Artificial foods can hinder the body's ability to heal itself. Maximize opportunities to use fresh foods. Add fresh bell pepper, onion/garlic, and celery to not only soups, stews, and gravies but also to other fresh or frozen vegetables. The first replacement for fresh foods should be frozen foods and then canned foods. Frozen foods may have been picked and then immediately frozen, whereas canned foods lose nutrients while in the can, which could be a lengthy time. Also, minimize your family's fast-food consumption. Fast foods can contain artificial ingredients and possibly hormones. Whole fresh foods should always be the first and best alternative.

Plan a healthy, nutritional, and economical menu with your child by age eight or before. Prepare foods of various colors. When planning a meal choose at least two vegetables—one green, one light colored—and a protein. A few other good options include vegetable and protein stews, casseroles, soups, or beans. The food pyramid would be a good concept to explain.

Dr. Renee M. Turchi, who does hunger research at St. Christopher's Hospital in Philadelphia, Pennsylvania, says, "Nutrition is vital for brain growth in the first three years of life…and lack of food can stunt the size and wiring of kids' brains. Poorly nourished children can have delays in development that affect IQ. While experts say most hungry Americans will not starve to death, people who don't have enough food, and enough of the right food, will not thrive—a condition called food insecurity."

Mariana Chilton, professor at Drexel University School of Public Health, says, "By ninth grade, many students who haven't had enough food during their lives become disengaged, with no sense of the future. They begin taking risks—the boys becoming violent, the girls getting pregnant. Then the cycle starts again. Even if a child younger than three is deprived of proper nutrition for just a week here or there, it has a detrimental, immediate effect on the brain when it's building connections like crazy" (Chilton 2010).

There could be a link between ADD/ADHD—attention deficit disorder or attention deficit hyperactivity disorder—and artificial coloring, artificial sweeteners, and preservatives. More studies are needed. If your child has been diagnosed, check with your child's pediatrician or a dietician to learn about natural remedies for ADD/ADHD.

Dr. Valine B. Hewitt, FACC, says in her article in *Life Links*, "The Nutritious, Delicious Way to Go Red, Are Red Dyes Dangerous?" "The color red may occur naturally in produce, but that's not always the case with packaged foods. Manufacturers sometimes add red dye to make foods and drinks appear more appetizing and fun. The Food and Drug Administration considers these additives safe. But there's evidence they may trigger behavior problems, such as lack of attention and hyperactivity, in some children. The American Academy of Pediatrics (AAP) says the evidence is weak. AAP experts don't recommend special diets for treating behavior problems. However, other researchers raise concerns about the way dyes affect chemicals around the brain. Dyes have become much more common in recent years, they note, increasing exposure. So should children steer clear? A parent or grandparent can talk with a child's doctor about any sensitivities and allergies. In most cases, eliminating a type of food won't harm a child and might help."

Dr. Alan Greene, Pediatrician, believes there is a definite link between food dye additives and ADHD and other child behavioral problems. He says one serving of artificial dyes can trigger behavioral problems. The good news is he believes that after abstaining from these dyes, you may see an improvement in behavior within one week.

As well as ADD/ADHD, more study should be done on possible links between depression and chemicals like artificial coloring and other additives in our food.

It is most beneficial for family health to prepare and eat fresh vegetables and fruits daily and to eliminate artificial coloring, flavoring, sweeteners, and preservatives.

> *Let your food be your medicine and*
> *your medicine be your food.*
> —Imhotep, an ancient Egyptian doctor,
> mathematician, and architect

TIP NUMBER SEVENTEEN
Engage in Family Activities

Participate in family-oriented activities at home, for example: board games (Candy Land, Pictionary, Monopoly, Scrabble, Chess, Checkers, Sequence, Guesstures, Taboo, etc.), card games (War, Old Maid, Uno, 500 Gin Rummy, Tonk, Pinochle, etc.), musical-instrument sessions, singing and dancing, outdoor activities (picnics, concerts, social events as birthday parties, dinners, etc.), and so on. Take your child roller skating, ice skating, bowling, skiing, etc. on a regular basis.

Family fun and belonging will be satisfied. Having fun together strengthens family ties and bonds. These activities also teach your child how to spend their spare time and they provide fun ways to stay physically active. Fun activities will be passed along to your child's family in the future.

When engaging with family activities, valuable lessons can be taught on being a good winner and a good loser. Losing should not be associated with the child as an individual and his or her self-worth. Separate the child from his or her performance.

Together, you can make an action plan to improve performance, with the child making most of the suggestions. Give the child credit when the plan works. Winning should be handled with a feeling of accomplishment, with humility, and with empathy. Teach your child that being able to make a valuable contribution is most important.

> *The stronger the youngster's sense of personal worth, the more secure he feels in his group, the easier it is for him to base his decisions on personal conviction rather than on the need for group approval. The lower his self-respect, the less he belongs, the stronger the temptation to go along with group pressures to win a place for himself.*
> —Dorothy Corkille Briggs, *Your Child's Self-Esteem*

Development of spirituality and praying together as a family is uplifting and powerful. I believe a family that prays together stays together.

Note: Parents should never have the child choose or take sides between parents. Keep your child out of parental fights and disagreements. He or she will internalize negativity.

Having fun and communicating as a family leads to healthy feelings of belonging (Tip Number Two). Without a sense of family belonging, your child will seek other groups of which to belong, which could be a gang, a cult, or marginal people.

TIP NUMBER EIGHTEEN

Encourage School and Community Activities

Enroll your child in school and community activities, such as little-league baseball, basketball, soccer, football, tennis, track, golf, and Ping-Pong; science, math, and engineering classes; and art classes, dance classes, voice lessons, and instrument lessons. Select the activity in which your child seems to show the most interest and performs effortlessly. Exercise and physical activity is physically and mentally beneficial in maintaining weight and mental sharpness.

Teach your child that believing in themselves is half the battle; if they can conceive it, they can believe it, and they can achieve it. They should learn that everyone has failures, but don't fear failure, and don't let failure define who you are. Failure is only temporary. Practice, preparation, and belief in yourself are the best defenses against failure. Another way to look at failure is that failure can be a stepping stone from which to learn and from which to catapult to success. Teach your child to keep trying, striving, and visualizing success.

> *Lots of people limit their possibilities by giving up easily. Never tell yourself this is too much for me. It's no use. I can't go on. If you do you're licked, and by your own thinking too. Keep believing and keep on keeping on.*
> —Dr. Norman Vincent Peale

During activities, find examples to teach and communicate team cooperation and what being a fair team player is and represents. Here is an opportunity to teach the Golden Rule: *"Do unto others as you would have them do unto you."* Teach your child that every effort given in good faith is a good effort and well worth it.

> *You've got to get to the stage in life where going for it is more important than winning or losing.*
> —Arthur Ashe

Have your child find an opportunity to do something for someone else in the community. Your child can run errands, volunteer to work on political campaigns, tutor younger children, volunteer at a community center, mentor other children, and so on. Volunteering his or her time is an opportunity for your child to give back, which builds self-worth and trustworthiness. You can also plan a trip to a prison, drug-abuse program, hospital, or the like and discuss the detriment of using drugs and alcohol. This is also an opportunity to have your child contribute the culmination of his or her learning to society, which leads to healthier thriving (Tip Number Two).

> *There is nothing more dangerous than to build a society with a large segment of people in that society who feel that they have no stake in it; who feel that they have nothing to lose. People who have stake in their society, protect that society, but when they don't have it, they unconsciously want to destroy it.*
> —Rev. Dr. Martin Luther King, Jr.

The benefits here include physical and mental strengthening, building personal character and family bonds, and contributing to society.

TIP NUMBER NINETEEN

Encourage Musical-Instrument Participation

E ncourage your child to play a musical instrument or participate in school musical programs (orchestra, band, choir, etc.) and other school extracurricular activities.

Being able to simultaneously handle the school curriculum and extracurricular activities (including other school activities such as class government, gardening, the school newspaper, and Young Achievers Organization), is a beneficial skill to develop. This skill can be also transferred to other scenarios.

Children who play musical instruments do better in school. Using every part of the brain expands a person's ability to take in larger amounts of information and knowledge. In the1990's, scientific studies were done on the effect of children hearing classical music such as Mozart on increasing intelligence and cognition. Don Campbell's *Mozart Effect: Tapping the Power of Music to Heal the Body, Strengthen the Mind, and Unlock the*

Creative Spirit, Avon Books, 1997, stated that playing classical music, such as Mozart, improves the performance of certain mental tasks and improves the overall ability of babies to learn. I suggest that the music of jazz greats such as Count Basie and Duke Ellington can be substituted for the music of Mozart to obtain similar results.

While your child is eating meals, is sleeping or napping, or is playing, play instrumental or orchestral music in the background from the radio, stereo, TV channel, CD, digital streaming, and so forth. Take your child to musical concerts and plays to expand his or her musical appreciation and development. Your child will subconsciously develop an appreciation for the music.

Music appreciation can be a bridge to happiness, can stimulate learning, and can nurture the soul.

TIP NUMBER TWENTY
Give Your Child Responsibility

Make your child responsible by giving him or her responsibility. Your child should have regular weekly household chores. These chores should be within your child's ability and be previously taught with a clear explanation of the task and an example and expectation of how the finished product should look. Assign chores with a reasonable start and finish time or date. Give your child enough time to complete each chore. Everything is learned. Children learn to work when given an opportunity to work. Laziness is also learned when no or low expectations are given. As Adler says, contributing leads to healthier thriving (Tip Number Two).

Taking care of a pet is an opportunity to teach responsibility by having your child exclusively care for their pet—feeding, walking, and disposing of feces. Watering house plants can be another responsibility.

Give your child the responsibility of taking care of his or her own possessions, such as a bicycle, games, toys, and tools, and so forth. Provide a storage place where your child is responsible for returning items after use. Teach your child to value his or her property; you will spend less money when you don't have to replace the mistreated or damaged property. Money can be limited, and when you spend money replacing an item, you have less money to spend on other wanted or needed items. If your child forgets and property is damaged or lost, do not replace the item. Calmly and lovingly, let your child know that he or she should replace it with his or her allowance or replace it by getting paid through "**money opportunities**" (described below). Having your child replace the item is a form of logical consequences (Tip Number Three). We take more care of something we know may not be replaced without our personal effort.

When I was approximately six years old, I visited a family whose daughter had a paint set with an easel. I dipped the brush in all the colors without rinsing first, ruining the individual colors. It was not intentional; no one had taught me how to use it. The girl was upset and began to say I had ruined her paint set. My dad said that I would have to replace it with my allowance. I sacrificed an allowance, and I have never ruined anyone's property since.

If your child's property needs to be replaced, work with your child to decide on a plan to replace the item. A plan could be to pay your child extra for doing special chores that you would outsource. Name it "money opportunities." Designate chores with a commensurate amount of money paid for each. Predetermine specific tasks with money amounts and have your child choose which chore he or she would like to perform. Money opportunities can be paid according to the difficulty of a task. The more difficult the task, the more money the child will receive.

Money opportunities are not regular weekly chores such as making beds, watering the plants, taking out trash, cleaning their room, cleaning bathrooms, and washing dishes, for which an allowance would suffice. Money opportunities, depending on your child's age and ability, could be helping your child plan and start a business where money can be earned, such as a lemonade stand, babysitting, shoveling snow, raking leaves, running errands, and washing cars. Your child can also sell something he or she likes or makes, something in which he or she excels, or something your child can do effortlessly, such as organizing children's parties, serving as a DJ for a party, making greeting cards, teaching computer technology to neighborhood kids, tutoring, or producing website designs.

Help your child calculate and determine his or her profit by writing down and adding all money earned (revenue), then subtracting money spent for expenditures (lemons, sugar, cups, sign, lawn mower, rake, shovel, soap, music, paper, ink, "sweat equity," etc.), to determine profit or "bottom line." Profit should be put back into the business. Real profit, or operating in the "black" instead of operating in the "red" (without profit), may not be achieved for the first two years. Operating as a business is an opportunity for your child to learn, culminate, and improve their life skills. For your information, the term "Black Friday" refers to the day when a company can generate enough sales for the company's accountant to use black ink instead of red ink to indicate a profit from sales.

When starting a **business with low risk** (which indicates you are less likely to be sued by a customer)—such as a lawn service, maid service, computer services, DJ service, tutoring, selling greeting cards, and selling other imperishable items—applying for a **sole-proprietorship** type of ownership will suffice. To be a legally operating company as a sole proprietorship, you need adult status. A parent can acquire for their child an **Employer Identification Number (EIN)**, which can be gotten from your Internal Revenue Service; and a **Fictitious Name application**, which can be gotten by calling the Fictitious Name Bureau in your state capitol. If your child has developed a one-of-a-kind product or service, you may need to register it for **patent or copyright** protection. If the product/service has been used by consumers for more than one year, it is considered "public domain" and legal protection cannot be acquired. You can consult a patent attorney. You may also need **trademark or logo** protection. Call The Library of Congress, Washington, DC for information and for an application. You may also go on the internet to obtain the above applications.

A sole proprietorship is easy to set up; however, you can lose your personal assets if the business fails or if legal action is taken against the company. If you **incorporate** (preferably Limited Liability Company or LLC), you will **not** lose your personal assets if the company fails or if legal action is taken against the company. Incorporation is usually applied for through an attorney; the EIN and Fictitious Name clearance is acquired with the **Certificate of Incorporation**. The attorney will also inform you of other documents needed when incorporating.

Instill in your child the need and benefit of owning the businesses in your community. There is self respect, self worth, and control in being your own boss through business ownership. If the business owner has a stake in the community in which he or she lives or operates, he or she will uplift the community by paying taxes, which maintain and support community public goods and infrastructure; by providing employment opportunities; by providing training programs; by providing school scholarships; by providing support of community sports teams; and by providing role models for young people to emulate.

Help your child develop a solid work ethic, including producing and delivering a quality product or service, being on time, being truthful/honest, keeping deadlines, and continuing to develop his or her skills and knowledge. Teach your child that the quality of the product or service is as important as their profit or bottom line. The goal is to make a profit, but it should also be to develop quality, honesty, and integrity.

To develop additional knowledge and competency in your child, you can enroll your child in various night classes, weekend programs, or summer programs in business, science, technology, engineering, math, or arts. This will be worth the money, especially if the cost is reasonable.

Encourage your child to volunteer his or her time toward a political election, at a public library, or shopping for an elderly neighbor. Discuss what they learned and the advantages and disadvantages of their efforts. This can also help to eliminate summer-learning stagnation, and it provides constructive ways to spend a child's spare time.

When a child is fifteen or sixteen (or before), a part-time job, volunteering, or interning in a career area of his or her choice is very beneficial. Interacting with your child over the years should have given you insight into the areas in which your child excels—something your child does well and does effort-lessly. Encourage your child to select a profession that brings him or her the intrinsic rewards of inner satisfaction and peace. In the early years, encourage your child to work for free. The salary is not the most important thing; the experience and the development of skill-sets are. This is what Robert Kiyosaki, author of *Rich Dad, Poor Dad*, did. As a child, he worked for free acquiring many skill-sets to eventually become a millionaire.

Your child's first job may require **working papers** for paren-tal and governmental consent. Check to make sure state and federal government guidelines for children at work and child safety laws are followed. Working papers can be acquired from your child's high school.

Childhood patterns follow into adulthood. If you are not made to or not taught to work or make a valuable contribution at an early age, you will be less likely to have a desire to work and contribute at a later age. Start your child early in the direction you want him or her to go. Laziness is taught and learned when a child is not given a work alternative or opportunity.

Good luck with teaching your child to drive. Alternatives could be a drivers' education class at school or in the local commu-nity. Car insurance discounts for your child could result from having previous driver's lessons for your child and your child's school grade point average (GPA) of B and above.

The individual who can do something that the world wants done will, in the end, make his way regardless of his race.
—Booker T. Washington

TIP NUMBER TWENTY-ONE
Encourage Journal Writing

Encourage your child to write down his or her thoughts in a journal. Remind your child to bring the journal on various trips. When traveling (though not while in motion), have your child write down experiences, thoughts, and feelings along the way. Before long, your child should begin to enjoy writing down his or her thoughts. You are building writing skills and reading skills through contextual application. When a skill or knowledge is taught with real-life application from the child's viewpoint, mastery of the skill is more likely.

Journaling is also a good way for your child to identify, visualize, and articulate their goals in writing. Creating and forming a mental image of specific and desired goals and accomplishments with benchmarks—dates by which desired outcomes are to be accomplished—is powerful and more easily worked toward when put into writing.

Have your child write and send postcards and thank-you notes to friends and family members. This strengthens family ties, strengthens literacy, and teaches your child to show appreciation and gratitude for kind gestures shown to him or her.

Start an early routine with your child to make or buy birthday and holiday cards for the other spouse and parent. You will appreciate it when your child continues these patterns for a lifetime and you are the benefactor. This is a great opportunity to have your child give back and, as a result, helps in developing self-worth, self-validation, trust, and trustworthiness, all of which translate into sound emotional health.

Periodically, send a note of encouragement to your child through your child's favorite mode of technological communication—for example, cell phone, e-mail, text, Facebook, Twitter, and Instagram. You never know when your child is on the brink of something that your encouragement can help bring them through. Words of caution—do not give too many messages; overdoing it can seem insincere or untruthful.

Pen pals are also nice to have. Parents should know all pen pals and keep communication open among all parties, with the parents in the forefront.

> *Dare to be more than you thought you could be.*
> —Dr. Maya Angelou

TIP NUMBER TWENTY-TWO

Encourage Learning a
Foreign Language

Encourage your child to learn a foreign language as early as possible. The younger the child the better potential for internalization. Your child's overall intelligence will improve, and bilingual brains deteriorate more slowly than monolingual brains.

Speaking an additional language can also heighten a child's self-worth because he or she can do something few of his or her peers can do. Developing friendships with people who speak another language can be beneficial to contributing to world peace and awareness. Help select a pen pal from another country with your child. Speaking a foreign language can also later be beneficial when seeking employment, volunteering, or interning.

While your child is eating breakfast or another meal, playing technology, TV stations, or radio channels of another language being spoken or sung is helpful. Using the library or taking classes at school (day or evening) are options as well.

We live in a global society; all countries in the world are interconnected. The ability to speak another language affords the power to bridge communication barriers, form foreign alliances, and enhance self-esteem.

TIP NUMBER TWENTY-THREE
Attend School Open House

Attend your child's school open house, parent-teacher conferences, special events, extracurricular activities, and sports activities at school on a regular basis. This is an opportunity for you as parents to be enlightened on school policy and school rules, to be enlightened on school curriculum and programs, and to be enlightened on your child's academic and social progress. You can also make periodic, unannounced visits to your child's school to check your child's progress. If possible, accompany your child on the first day of school to meet your child's teachers. You know your child better than anyone else. If necessary, communicate to your child's teacher his or her strengths, weaknesses, and positive and negative ways of learning.

Do not do your child's schoolwork or homework for him or her. Your child will miss the opportunity to develop important foundational skills like managing start-time and due-date requirements, research skills, and paper-preparation skills, all of which lead to your child's proficiency, self-satisfaction, and internal rewards. Your child is also developing skills and proficiencies that can be transferred to other projects and situations.

Parents communicate values through their actions. Where you show interest is what your child will think is important. Your child will value education and school as a result of your actions. Also, teachers treat students better when they know and communicate with their parents. Teachers are more conscious of their actions when there is accountability to parents. Let's face it: positive relationships among teachers, parents, and student are win-win-win situations.

TIP NUMBER TWENTY-FOUR
Teach Your History

Teach your child his or her own history by sharing the cultural accomplishments and achievements from your family's past and present. Teach your child your traditional ethnic and cultural language, dances, mores, and customs. Read and provide cultural history books on the positive contributions made by your people—contributions that may not be provided by your child's school.

> *My people are destroyed from lack of knowledge.*
> —The Bible, New International Version,
> Hosea 4:6

We all have a need to be positively recognized. This can be obtained through books and family ties. Your family history and ancestry is your foundation and can be your greatest feeling of belonging if it is hospitable and respectful. If you do not define yourself, others will define you—perhaps in a negative way. Teach your child your definition of who they are.

History is a light that illuminates the past and
a key that unlocks the door to the future.
—Dr. Runoko Rashidi

We develop our self-esteem through interaction with our parents; we develop our race-esteem through knowledge of our racial history.

When an elder dies, it's like a library
has been burned to the ground.
—African Proverb

The relationship of a people to their history is the
same as the relationship of a child to its mother.
—Dr. John Henrik Clarke

The task before Africans both at home and
abroad is to restore to their memory what slav-
ery and colonialism made us forget.
—Dr. John Henrik Clarke

Tony Brown gives an example of how others' misconceptions of a people can affect them:

Through the decades, the Black image has been ridiculed
and vilified in popular American culture and exploited for
the commercial benefit of Whites. The Black stereotype has
been reinforced and spread around the world in films and
on radio and television….Blacks have been dehumanized as
coons, brutes, mammies, shuffling darkies, predators, and

> *sex fiends. Today's Black gangsta culture embraces those stereotypes and sings their praises in rap form, glorifying sociopathic behavior. How would you like to be a Black child growing up in that environment? Under this psychological barrage, nearly all Blacks wind up psychologically damaged to some extent by corrupted images and low self-esteem.*
> —Tony Brown

Television and movies offer unrealistic scenarios that are detrimental for family and for individuals in the African American community to imitate and emulate.

> *When you control a man's thinking, you do not have to worry about his actions. You do not have to tell him not to stand here or go yonder. He will find his "proper place" and will stay in it. You do not need to send him to the back door. He will go without being told. In fact, if there is no back door, he will cut one for his special benefit. His education makes it necessary.*
> —Dr. Carter G. Woodson

Have family reunions on a regular basis—once a year or once every two years. As an activity, you can give each member an assignment on a topic to present to others. It could revolve around family-tree information or cultural knowledge and awareness. If you know who you are, you are more likely to know where you are going. I have known people who were emotionally stunted because they did not know their biological lineage and connections.

When I discover who I am, I'll be free.
—Ralph Ellison

Africans came to America, BEFORE, DURING AND AFTER enslavement. Don't start our history at the end; start it at the beginning.
—Dr. Runoko Rashidi

What you do for yourself, in large measure, depends on what you think of yourself. So if you think that you have no worthy history, that you come from nothing, you will tend to act that out. But, if you think that you come from greatness, you will aim for the stars.
—Dr. Runoko Rashidi

Please refer to the suggested *Ethnic Book Resources* in this book.

TIP NUMBER TWENTY-FIVE
Display Standard Treatment

Treat your child the way you would expect others to treat him or her. Your treatment will become the standard for the way your child feels others should also treat them. *Treat your child as if he or she already is what you want him or her to be, and through your efforts, your child will become what he or she ought to be.* State your expectations for them in positive terms. For example, it should be stated, "**When** you go to college...." not "**If** you go to college....."

We find out who we are from our parents, and then we make our own self-fulfilling prophecies from messages received from parents and others. Depending on whom we think we are, we put behaviors into place to become this identity and maintain it. People who allow others to abuse them think less of themselves and are more likely to have been abused in the past. We seek the familiar—what we know—whether right or wrong. We fear the unknown, whether right or wrong.

Input from parents determines the messages about ourselves that we play in our head, which will determine character (the foundation of who we are), which determines our conduct (our outward behavior). Refer to the Iceberg Analogy from Tip Number Three. We become and act the way we think we are—a self-fulfilling prophecy.

If we have been mistreated, we learn to mistreat others. Victims will make others their victims. When trust is violated, expect to be looked at with a jaundiced eye or with suspicion for a while, until trust can be restored.

We all have a need to have confirmation and affirmation of our worth and value within the family, within the community, and the world. Everyone has a need to be seen, heard, and valued. When you compliment your child, when you spend quality and quantity time with your child, when your eyes light up when your child comes into the room, and when you pleasantly acknowledge your child, it helps your child to build an armor of protection against negative self-feelings when others may say things to insult them, when failures come, and when rejection occurs.

Negative self-feelings, poor self-esteem, and poor self-concept can lead to self-destruction. *How you perceive yourself (and therefore the future) shapes your present behavior.* Effective parenting can help prevent drug use and addiction. People with alcohol and drug addictions, people who self-mutilate, and people who are bullies usually have negative self-feelings and low self-esteem, which leads to making the wrong decisions and judgments about themselves and the future.

The family should be your child's center of the universe, where he or she feels valued, capable, and loved. The more love one is able to give, the more love that comes back. The more one gives, the more one receives. The effort is worth the outcome. Remember: no good deed should go unnoticed.

If a child feels wounded, mistreated, or other injustices leading to destructive entitlement (Tip Number Three), **healing** will begin when the child is **given credit**—recognized or acknowledged for withstanding unfairness or sustaining abuse and persevering. Healing also will begin when the child is given an opportunity to **give back to others** in a similar situation. Give credit by saying, "I'm really sorry that happened to you. Sometimes bad things happen to good people," "I admire how you kept your cool while being mistreated; you didn't deserve that," or "It's not what someone does or says to you but how you respond to it, and you responded well and with dignity." Encourage a victim to help others in a similar situation by mentoring, spending time volunteering, fundraising, and so on. Healing takes place when credit is given to the victim for the wrong done and when the victim is able to help someone else in a similar situation.

Never withdraw love as a strategy to change negative behavior. No healing takes place without feeling loved. Refer to Tip Number Three. Remember to treat your child as if he or she already is what you want him or her to be, and through your efforts, your child will become what he or she ought to be.

Teach your child that sexual activity has a higher meaning and that emotional attachment and love should precede sexual activity. In doing so, your child should be less likely to be persuaded to have sex before he or she is ready. I have observed that women who have not received validation and enough attention and affection from their fathers are more likely to crave attention and affection from men by wearing provocative and sexy clothing to attract attention, and they are more willing to exchange what they need (attention, affection, validation, and love) for sex that the man wants. These women will seek validation and affirmation from every man in which they come in contact, not understanding the basis or cause of their behavior. This is an example of "looking for love in all the wrong places."

Before becoming sexually intimate and considering marriage, a young person should have met his or her significant other's family and know his or her religious affiliation (if any), credit score, marital past, number of children, education, criminal past (if any), employment status, salary, and veracity. I feel it is a responsibility to our future children to carefully select a mate who will be a good parent and spouse; do not ignore warning signs or red flags that indicate insincerity, lack of commitment, or low morals.

I would tell my students that love, commitment, marriage, and then children should happen in that order for their best interest. Through observation, I believe this order works better than getting married too young, having sex too early, or picking the wrong spouse. If you live your life out of order, your life will feel out of sync, and you will not be as productive because of unnecessary distractions, burdens, and responsibilities. Teach your child that he or she should have a plan for his or her life with goals, timeframes, and expectations rather than just letting life happen. Live your life with purpose.

If your child has been molested or raped, do not treat the child's sexual abuse lightly; the effects can last for a lifetime without professional therapy. Teach your child about "good touch" and "bad touch," and, depending on your child's age, how to identify sexual grooming and seduction techniques. Tell your child that sexual abuse could feel good because of the attention and contact shown; however, it is harmful to developing healthy sexual boundaries and patterns. Tell your child that he or she should not have any secrets and to let you know if anyone suggests keeping secrets. Provide a fun environment for cousins and friends to feel comfortable and visit.

Protect your child by not letting your child go to or spend the night at other's homes, with the exception of some grandparents. Never put your child in a potential harmful situation. Thoroughly investigate any environment in which your child will be. The effects of sexual abuse can manifest as obesity, alcohol abuse, drug abuse, promiscuity, unhealthy attachments, and making others victims at the same age of their abuse. I call this last manifestation the *Dracula Syndrome*.

> *Some children who have been sexually abused equate love with sex and abuse because their boundaries have been violated. There are feelings of guilt and shame instead of a thriving self-worth. Add the likelihood of poverty, and by the time these girls are approached by a trafficker, many are desperate not only for someone who can provide food, clothing and shelter but also affection.*
> —YouthSpark, Inc. Reports

*The pimps' jobs have become much easier because some-
body's already groomed these children for this life. Seventy
to 90 percent of these girls have already been abused
in what is supposed to be the safety of their homes.*
—Dalia Racine, DeKalb County Assistant District
Attorney, GA

Treat your child as a precious jewel to be valued, protected, and enhanced, and your child will beam with self-respect, reciprocity, and dignity.

TIP NUMBER TWENTY-SIX

Provide Knowledge of Personal Finances

Educate your child about personal finances and money-market funds. Knowledge is power, and educating your child about financial matters will create an environment that promotes positive financial decision making and success. It is imperative that you teach your child how to spend his or her money. The younger the child is when learning, the more likely he or she is to retain the information and make money-wise decisions. It is most effective when money-wise decisions are modeled. Don't feel intimidated when thinking about finances. The following suggested concepts should be introduced to your child when needed and as age-appropriate.

> *The history of civilization shows that no people can well rise to a high degree of mental or even moral excellence without wealth.*
> —Frederick Douglass

Allow your child to make small decisions concerning his or her finances; however, be involved until proficient independence is shown. Help your child determine and **set priorities** for himself or herself depending on the **child's age, money available, personal needs, and wants**. Also, help your child make decisions about what goals to work toward. Have your child calculate and determine what to buy based on how long it would take to save the money needed, taking into consideration the law of supply and demand.

The **law of supply and demand** says that when people are purchasing **(demand)** a product or service, the **price will likely go up**. When people are not purchasing **(demand is down)** a product or service, the **price will likely go down**. When **supply** (quantity of product or service) is **up**, the **price will likely go down**, and when **supply is down**, the price will likely go **up** (e.g., the best price time to buy a lawn mower is in the fall, when demand is down, and the best price time to buy fruits is at their harvest season, when supply is up).

Take part in a **consumer-research process** with your child in order to locate the best practical product available for a purchase (e.g., using ConsumerReports.com or Bluebook.com). Calculate how long it would take to save enough money over time to buy the item. For example: If the item cost $59.99; allowance is $5 a week; it would take twelve weeks to save enough money. ($59.99 divided by 5 = 12) If the allowance is $10, it would take six weeks to save enough money. ($59.99 divided by 10 = 6)

Talk about the difference between spending for his or her **needs** (expenditures for survival—food, clothing, shelter), which is paid for with our **disposable income**, and spending for his or her **wants** (expenditures for comfort, pleasure, and entertainment), which is paid for with our **discretionary income**. Teach your child to identify and prioritize his or her **needs** first and then his or her **wants**.

I have observed a pattern with some people who have less discretionary income (designated for pleasure, comfort, and entertainment) and less disposable income (designated for shelter, food, and clothing). They replace property more often because they don't take proper care of property owned. When you spend money replacing property of which you don't take care, you have less money to spend on other items needed or wanted (e.g., a computer, a baseball glove, or lunch with a friend). There is a belief that people don't respect what they don't earn.

When shopping with your child, teach him or her how to **calculate the amount of change** to be returned to them. If the price of an item is one dollar and you paid with a five-dollar bill, allow your child to do the math him or herself by counting from two dollars up to five dollars. If the price is sixty-eight cents and the amount of payment given is one dollar, start counting by pennies from sixty-nine cents to seventy cents, then a nickel to count to seventy-five cents, and a quarter to count up to one dollar.

Enlighten your child about the concept of **haggling**, in which they can use cash and negotiate with vendors or independent merchants for a lower price for items.

Help your child prepare a **budget** based on his or her present allowance or income and their expenses or expenditures. Subtract expenses/expenditures based on the child's needs from total income/allowance and then determine the money available (net income) to be saved, invested or spent for wants. Encourage your child to save at least 10 percent of his or her total (net) income for investment or for an emergency fund. An emergency fund or rainy-day fund is necessary to save nine months to a year's income in case of unemployment to pay for expenses. You can give an incentive to save his or her money by matching the dollars they save. It is financially smarter to invest in real estate, gold, silver, platinum, or palladium than saving in a bank. Acquiring diamonds, sapphires, emeralds, and rubies are also good. The value of real estate and aforementioned metals/gems will appreciate (go up) at a faster rate than the interest rate provided by a bank for holding your money. If you decide to save your money in a bank or credit union, make sure the institution is secured by the **FDIC** (Federal Deposit Insurance Corporation). Also, you can set a pattern for your child to contribute a small portion of what they earn to the family's budget. Contributions to family budget set a precedent for contributing to their future family. Also, have respect for your child's money and other possessions by not taking what belongs to your child without permission or negotiation. Give the same consideration as you would want to be treated.

Total Income (Revenue)
– Expenditures for needs
Net Income—Money left over for wants, savings, or investments

Talk about the difference between a **credit card**, which is borrowing money from a lender or money agent (bank or credit union) and a **debit card**, which is using your own money held by a money agent (bank or credit union), hopefully with interest paid to you. Paying with a credit card usually will cost you more money due to interest-rate charges than paying with a debit card. If using a credit card is necessary, first-month full payment is usually needed to avoid interest charges. Inquire with your bank about points that can be earned with a credit card toward money back or gifts. Wisely, don't spend more than what can be paid for in full the following month. Don't use your credit card for everyday expenses. However, paying with a debit card may be beneficial to avoid debt and interest charges, and your account could earn interest. A debit card is usually linked with a **checking account** (demand payment account) when checks can be written to pay a debt or issue payment. By the time your child exits high school, he or she should be familiar with a checkbook, its parts (checks, register, and deposit clips), how to write a check, and how to balance monthly debits and credits. Teach your child to spend less than he or she makes in salary, and inform him or her about local, state, and federal income-tax deductions. **Gross income** (hours worked times rate per hour) minus all taxes and other deductions equals **net income**. For example: 40 hours/week X rate per hour ($10) = $400/Gross income; $400 minus $100/taxes and other deductions equals $300/net income.

Teach your child about interest rate charges on loans as well as the benefit of earning interest on money saved through a savings account. Let your child know that a **FICO score** (Fair, Isaac and Company) can affect a credit interest-rate charge. A higher FICO score of 720 and above means a lower interest rate charged on a credit card and loan interest rate. Negotiation of a zero interest rate is possible with a credit score of eight hundred and over. A high FICO score is obtained by paying bills on time and paying more than the minimum amount due. It is best to borrow less than 30 percent of your credit limit and to pay the entire amount at the end of the month. It is also determined by your salary-to-debt ratio (you should make enough to pay your bills comfortably), the number of credit cards you have, the maximum credit amount allowed, and length of time employed. You can find your credit score by contacting Experian, TransUnion, or Equifax. Collateral and a cosigner should not be necessary with a good FICO score.

A **cosigner** is a person who agrees to pay if the original purchaser defaults (fails to pay) on payment. **Collateral** is when a person gives something of value to a creditor (lender) to secure the loan. My dad cosigned for me when I bought my first new automobile for $2,000. Even though I had proven myself to be responsible by paying a small amount of rent each month, I realized later that he took a significant risk for my benefit. After I was able to establish a solid credit history, I did not need a cosigner or collateral. I had earned my right to be independent.

My husband acquired a credit rating (FICO score); when he finished high school, he took out a loan from a bank for $300. He didn't spend it; he just paid back the loan with the money borrowed in order to acquire a credit rating and credit reference. Also, obtaining a credit card from a bank with a small credit limit can be used for this purpose. Advise your child that they should not borrow until they have acquired permanent employment. They should want to make sure they can comfortably pay off the loan. Full payment within thirty days is best for your FICO score and best to eliminate interest charges. Defaulting (not being able to make a payment) will lower a FICO score and will add additional penalty charges to the amount owed. Explain to your child the detriment of defaulting on payment and its long-term effects.

Be as creative as your imagination and expertise will allow when teaching financial lessons to your child. After I graduated from high school and showed my family I could be financially responsible, my dad and my mom gave me a gold watch that cost sixty dollars. My dad said I would have to pay the jeweler one-half the cost of the watch. I was furious because I knew he could afford to pay the entire amount. Without my knowing, my dad negotiated with the jewelers that if I paid on time each month, I would be granted a credit card from them. I paid back five dollars a month for six months. Later, when I decided to open a department-store credit card, I was asked for credit references. I used the jeweler as a credit reference, and then I understood the gift my dad had given me. I realized it was more than the gift of credit; it was also the gift of being given responsibility, being able to follow through to an end result, being able to budget my personal finances, being able to exhibit consistent behavior patterns, and being able to acquire a feeling of accomplishment. When I acquired a full-time job and was living at home, I paid rent to my parents. It was only $100 a month; however, it was a valuable lesson to prepare me for future responsibilities.

Teach your child about **bank and credit union savings accounts, certificates of deposit, stocks, mutual funds, and treasury bills**, as well as the approximation of the interest rates for each. Interest rates will fluctuate depending on the economic market. Your assignment can be to investigate current interest rates with your child.

The **Rule of Seventy-two** is the method of estimating how long it would take for your investment to double the amount invested. Divide 72 by the interest percentage rate given. The quotient will tell you how many years it will take to double the money invested. Seventy-two (72) divided by three percent interest rate return equals 24 years to double the amount invested.

Return on Investment (ROI) is a way to calculate the return on investment. The benefit (return) of an investment is divided by the cost of the investment. The result is expressed as a percentage or a ratio. For example: $5,000 (return) divided by $10,000 (cost of investment) equals .50 percent

Let your child know that **reading the small print** on documents is essential, and list the consequences of not reading the small print (e.g., hidden balloon rates after a certain period of time, interest-only loans, minor changes that could be significant, and major changes in original contract terms after a certain period of time). Teach your child to avoid being taken advantage of due to lack of knowledge. Written agreements supersede oral agreements.

When money is lent or borrowed on a personal basis, creating a **promissory note** is advisable for protection against nonpayment. It is a written obligation to promise to pay a lender that states the money amount promised to pay, the names of people involved, and the payment terms (e.g., when payments begin, dates for increment of payments, and the length of time of debt).

Teach your child that in order for a **contract** to be valid and legally binding, the contract must consist of an offer and an acceptance of the terms, supported by legally sufficient consideration (giving something of value), of legal purpose, and made by parties who have the legal capacity (being sane and of adult age) to enter into the contract. There should be a "legal meeting of the minds." A written, legally binding contract will take precedence over an oral agreement. You may have to sign for a child not of legal age. Consult further with professional legal counsel.

Teach your child how to **effectively negotiate** for what you need and want with others. Show how single- or multiple-person decisions can be made with accordance and harmony. Once while I was walking down the street in Los Angeles with my lovely daughter, we overheard two men talking in front of us. One said to the other, "I see your point; however, I see it this way." And then he began to explain his point of view. The listener gave him the same respect by listening to his point of view, and then they both came to a compromise. My daughter and I looked at each other and expressed that it was an effective way to work through a negotiation process.

*A typical **negotiation process** includes answering these questions:*

- *What is your belief or attitude?*
- *What are the major elements of your argument?*
- *What is the opposing/alternative belief or attitude?*
- *What are the major elements of this alternative?*
- *What commonalities exist between the two viewpoints?*
- *What compromise can you agree upon?*

Eggland, et. al., *Introduction to Business*, Mason, OH: South Western Publishing, 2003.

An **IRA** (individual retirement account) is either a 401K for employees of privately owned companies (personal businesses) or a 403B for employees of publicly owned companies (government controlled). Individuals who are not part of an organization can also invest in an IRA account. It is a savings account with the government or private organization for your retirement that earns compound interest. **Compound interest** is when interest is computed on the amount saved plus the interest previously earned. For example, if your principal savings is $1,000 and interest is 6 percent, in the first year, $1,000 (principal savings) times 6 percent interest ($60) equals $1,060. In the second year, $1,060 (new principal savings) times 6 percent interest ($63.60) equals $1,123.60. In the third year, $1,123.60 (new principal savings) times 6 percent interest ($67.42) equals $1,191.02 new principal savings, and so on, until principal savings is withdrawn by you without penalty at a certain age. Keep in mind that your principal will also go even higher because of your continued contributions. When working for a company, ask if they are willing to match your regular IRA contributions. A **Roth IRA** may provide for more flexibility. Consult a financial advisor.

Teach your child about the differences in **renting, leasing, and buying property or land**. With leasing, you make installment payments with the possibility of buying later. The previous installment payments can be applied to the selling price. When renting, the monthly payments will not be retrieved. Buying property or land is the best decision among the three. It is beneficial in the long run because property will appreciate (go up in value and price) over time and should be worth more when sold or converted to cash. When buying and securing a loan for a mortgage, your FICO score is necessary to determine the best interest and principle rate for your mortgage payment. Permanent ownership, receiving a deed to a home or title to an automobile, will not take place until the last payment due is paid.

Teach the accounting principle: **"Assets = Liabilities + Capital. Assets/Owner's Equity"** **Assets** is the sum total if all capital is sold for cash and all debts were paid. **Liabilities** are debts owed to others—credit card balances, automobile loans, home mortgage, personal loans. **Capital** is valuables such as home and land owner's equity, money in bank accounts, investments, furniture, automobiles, antique comic books, gold, silver, cash, old coins, jewelry, clothing, collectible stamps, fifty-year-old toys preferably in the original box, or anything that can be converted to cash. These non-cash capital valuables have liquidity. **Liquidity** is how easy it is to quickly convert property and other valuables to cash with little consequence. An example of **Owner's Equity** is if you own a home worth $200,000, you owe $150,000 towards future mortgage payments, your home owner's equity is $50,000, which could be converted to cash by home refinancing or by sale of the home.

Teach children that donating or giving money contributions is a principle of the **"open hand theory."** With an open hand of giving, you will also have an open hand to receive blessings. Giving or contributing is the ultimate goal of Alfred Adler's Surviving/ Thriving Cycle (mentioned in Tip

Number Two). Remember that wanting to contribute is preceded by a feeling of Belonging (having been held, touched, hugged, kissed, played with, invited) and Learning (having been taught skills, encouraged to be self-reliant, been given little criticism, had mistakes accepted, had interest in our knowledge shown).

For maximum security and usage of your money, consult a financial advisor. The financial goal is to grow your money and to have more money coming to you than money going out. You should at least stay **solvent** (being able to pay your debts) and not **insolvent** (having more liabilities than assets). You also want to be able to pass wealth on to your child. Generational wealth can catapult your next generation into a more secured financial level and social status.

The 10 Wealth for Life Principles

1. I will live within my means.
2. I will maximize my income potential through education and training.
3. I will effectively manage my budget, credit, debt, and tax obligations.
4. I will save at least 10% of my income.
5. I will use homeownership as a foundation for building wealth.
6. I will devise an investment plan for my retirement needs and children's education.
7. I will ensure that my entire family adheres to sensible money management principles.

8. I will support the creation and growth of minority-owned businesses.
9. I will guarantee my wealth is passed on to future generations through proper insurance and estate planning.
10. I will strengthen my community through philanthropy.

We realize that our future lies chiefly in our own hands. We know that neither institution nor friends can make a race stand unless it has strength in its own foundation; that races like individuals must stand or fall by their own merit; that to fully succeed they must practice the virtues of self-reliance, self-respect, industry, perseverance, and economy.
—Paul Robeson

I would suggest reading a financial book(s) with your child. Here are some suggestions:

Rich Dad's Escape from the Rat Race: How to Become a Rich Kid by Following Rich Dad's Advice, by Robert T. Kiyosaki

Rich Dad Poor Dad: What the Rich Teach Their Kids About Money That the Poor and Middle Class Do Not!, by Robert T. Kiyosaki

Rich Kid Smart Kid: Giving Your Child a Financial Headstart, by Robert T. Kiyosaki

New Totally Awesome Money for Kids: Revised Edition (New Totally Awesome Series), by Arthur Bochner and Rose Bochner

It's Great to Be Grateful!: A Kids Guide to Being Thankful! (Elf-Help Books for Kids), by Michaelene Mundy and R. W. Alley

Money Sense for Kids, by Hollis Page Harman

Smart Money Smart Kids: Raising the Next Generation to Win with Money, by Dave Ramsey and Rachel Cruze

The Opposite of Spoiled: Raising Kids Who are Grounded, Generous, and Smart About Money, by Ron Lieber

Personal Guide: The Complete Beginner's Guide. A Simple Practical Approach to Making Money, Budgeting, Saving & Investing (Saving Investing Spending Debt Budget), by Craig Santoro

Blue Chip Kid: What Every Child (Parent) Should Know About Money, Investing, and the Stock Market, by David W. Bianchi

Critical Thinking & Warren Buffet Box Set: Make Smart Decisions Using This Simple Guidance and Remarkable Advice to Manage Your Work and Take Control, by Ava Young and David Brown

Penny to a Million: Junior Entrepreneur Guide, by Guy Incognito

Money Matters for Kids, by Larry Burkett

A Complete Guide to Personal Finance: For Teenagers, by Tamsen Butler

What All Kids (and Adults Too) Should Know About Saving and Investing, by Rob Pivnick

How to Save Money: Your Easy Guide with Tips on Budgeting and Saving Sustainable Cash for Kids, by Ria C. Newbold

Rich Kids: How to Raise Our Children to Be Happy and Successful In Life, by Tom Corley

You Can't Teach a Child to Ride a Bike at a Seminar, 2nd Edition: Sandler's 7-Step System for Successful Selling, by David Sandler and David Mattson

The Accounting Game: Basic Accounting Fresh from the Lemonade Stand, by Judith Orloff and Darrell Mullis

Teaching Kids About Money, Money Lessons for Kids, by Debbie Madson

EntreLeadership: Twenty Years of Practical Business Wisdom from the Trenches, by Dave Ramsey

Kids, Wealth, and Consequences: Ensuring a Responsible Financial Future for the Next Generation, by Richard R. Morris and Jayne R. Pearl

The Kid's Guide to Money: Earning It, Saving It, Growing It, Sharing It, by Steven Otfinoski

The Cartoon Introduction to Economics: Volume One, Microeconomics, by Yoram Bauman and Grady Klein

After reading this book, do not be dismayed because you didn't receive what you needed to propel you towards ultimate success. There is a saying; you cannot give what you never received

without a conscious decision to change patterns. Be enthusiastic about giving what you didn't receive. You now have the tools and knowledge to better prepare your child—who is your future legacy, for emotional, academic, social, financial, and moral success.

Note: Intelligence without compassion and respect for others is null and void; it means nothing. You must teach both—being smart as well as being respectful and dignified. When you use all twenty-six tips in a loving, fun way, the return on your investment in your child will be tripled. It will be a win-win-win situation.

My greatest joys in life are to see all my children happy and prosperous, to see my husband happy, and to have a previous student greet me with enthusiasm and tell me I was the reason for his or her success. God bless!

You may reach me at email, debkelx@aol.com.

Child Care Selection Criteria

- Look for a three (3) or four (4) stars, which is considered quality, posted sticker on or in a child care building issued by Keystone Stars to indicate compliance with a quality rating system. A one (1) or two (2) stars posting indicates that the quality of the child care is not as compliant with quality excellence of total environment with classroom, food served, toys, books, and teachers.

- Look for credentials of teachers. Teachers should be certified with a bachelor or a master degree, and assistant teachers should have an associate degree.

- Visit in advance the potential child care; sit and observe in the classroom for a half day before enrolling your child to see what transpires. Look at the interaction between teacher and children, look at the interaction between/among children, and look at the student transition between activities to another activity. Children should be happy with attentive staff. After enrollment, visit unannounced to see if the same quality is being followed.

- Look for a teacher/child ratio or proportion of one staff member for every four children for age birth to 1 year; one staff for every five children for ages 12 months to 24 months; one staff member for every six children for ages 24 months to 36 months; one staff member for every ten children for ages 3 years to 5 years

- Look for posted daily lesson plans for each day's cognitive learning and physical activities.

- Look for children's daily journal posted with pictures drawn by child expressing daily events, best part of the day, etc.

- An assessment of your child's abilities by the child care should be done within the first thirty days after enrollment to determine individual objectives and goals to be met by your child.

- The objective of a quality child care is your child's social, emotional, cognitive, and physical proficient development, and proficient preparation of learning-readiness skills for kindergarten.

Contributed by Michele Faison and Arlene Saunders, Precious Angels Child Care, Philadelphia, PA; Proprietors, Lawrence and Michele Faison

Book Quotations Plus

When an elder dies, it is like a library
burned to the ground.
—African Proverb

Identity determines activity.
— Chike Akua

Memory determines functional-
ity, value, speed, and capability.
—Chika Akua

Mind is the Master Power, it moulds and it makes; man is
mind, and forever more, he takes the tool of thought and
he fashioneth what he wills. He can bring forth a thousand
joys or a thousand ills. He thinks in secret and it comes
to pass; his environment is nothing but a looking glass.
—James Allen, *As A Man Thinketh*

*I've learned that people will forget what you
said, people will forget what you did, but people
will never forget how you made them feel.*
                                    —Dr. Maya Angelou

Dare to be more than you thought you could be.
                                    —Dr. Maya Angelou

*You've got to get to the stage in life where going for
it is more important than winning or losing.*
                                    —Arthur Ashe

My people are destroyed from lack of knowledge.
—The Bible, New International Version, Hosea 4:6

*Every child seeks and desires a self picture as capable
and strong, and behavior matches the self-image.
A basic rule about human behavior is that negative feelings exist before negative acts. We focus on
the act and ignore the feelings causing the act.*
—Dorothy Corkille Briggs, *Your Child's Self-Esteem*

*The stronger the youngster's sense of personal worth, the
more secure he feels in his group, the easier it is for him
to base his decisions on personal conviction rather than on
the need for group approval. The lower his self-respect,
the less he belongs, the stronger the temptation to go
along with group pressures to win a place for himself.*
                                    —Dorothy Corkille Briggs

*When you build friendly, warm, accepting relation-
ships with your children, you increase the chances that
they will give your values serious consideration.*
—Dorothy Corkille Briggs, *Your Child's Self-Esteem*

*The Black population in America has historically been
marginalized by the manipulation of images in the
media. Both Whites and Blacks have been conditioned
to believe that Whites are superior and Blacks inferior.
This has been accomplished by creating negative symbols
that define Blacks: poverty, crime, violence, unemployment, irresponsibility. In fact, Blacks are defined by their
problems. This is the tragedy of Blacks in America—that
the image is the message and the media is the image.*
—Tony Brown, *Black Lies, White Lies, The Truth
According to Tony Brown*

*Through the decades, the Black image has been ridiculed
and vilified in popular American culture and exploited for
the commercial benefit of Whites. The Black stereotype has
been reinforced and spread around the world in films and
on radio and television...Blacks have been dehumanized as
coons, brutes, mammies, shuffling darkies, predators, and
sex fiends. Today's Black gangsta culture embraces those
stereotypes and sings their praises in rap form, glorifying
sociopathic behavior. How would you like to be a Black child
growing up in that environment? Under this psychological
barrage, nearly all Blacks wind up psychologically damaged
to some extent by corrupted images and low self-esteem.*
—Tony Brown, *Black Lies, White Lies, The Truth
According to Tony Brown*

Parental engagement fostered around the dinner table is one of the most potent tools to help parents raise healthy, drug-free children.
—Joseph A. Califano Jr.

By ninth grade, many students who haven't had enough food during their lives become disengaged, with no sense of the future. They begin taking risks—the boys becoming violent, the girls getting pregnant. Then the cycle starts again. Even if a child younger than three is deprived of proper nutrition for just a week here or there, it has a detrimental, immediate effect on the brain when it's building connections like crazy.
—Mariana Chilton

Give a man a fish he will eat for a day. Teach a man to fish he will eat for a lifetime.
—Chinese Proverb

The relationship of a people to their history is the same as the relationship of a child to its mother.
—Dr. John Henrik Clarke

The task before Africans both at home and abroad is to restore to their memory what slavery and colonialism made us forget.
—Dr. John Henrik Clarke

Learning is doing, and doing is learning.
—John Dewey

*It's not what you call us, but what
we answer to that matters.*

—Djuka

*The history of civilization shows that no peo-
ple can rise to a high degree of mental or
even moral excellence without wealth.*
—Frederick Douglass

Truth is proper and beautiful in all times and in all places.
—Frederick Douglass

*One's work may be finished some-
day, but one's education never.*
—Alexander Dumas

When I discover who I am, I'll be free.
—Ralph Ellison

Fervor is the weapon of choice of the impotent.
—Frantz Fanon

Mastery of language affords remarkable power.
—Frantz Fanon

*Never forget where we came from and always
praise the bridges that carried you over.*
—Fannie Lou Hamer

Be skilled in speech so that you will succeed.
The tongue of a man is his sword and effec-
tive speech is stronger than all fighting.
—The Husia, sacred wisdom of ancient Egypt

Let your food be your medicine and
your medicine be your food.
—Imhotep, Egyptian physician, architect, and
mathematician

Education remains the key to both eco-
nomic and political empowerment.
—Barbara Jordan

Act out your convictions.
— Rev. Dr. Martin Luther King, Jr.

If a man is called to be a street sweeper, he should sweep
streets even as Michelangelo painted, or Beethoven composed
music, or Shakespeare wrote poetry. He should sweep streets
so well that all the hosts of heaven and earth will pause to
say, here lived a great street sweeper who did his job well.
— Rev. Dr. Martin Luther King, Jr.

If you can't fly, then run; if you can't run, then
walk; if you can't walk, then crawl; but what-
ever you do, you have to keep moving forward.
— Rev. Dr. Martin Luther King, Jr.

Injustice anywhere leads to injustice everywhere.
— Rev. Dr. Martin Luther King, Jr.

*Take the first step in faith. You don't have to see
the whole staircase, just take the first step.*
— Rev. Dr. Martin Luther King, Jr.

*There is nothing more dangerous than to build a
society with a large segment of people in that
society who feel that they have no stake in it; who
feel that they have nothing to lose. People who
have stake in their society, protect that society,
but when they don't have it, they uncon-
sciously want to destroy it.*
— Rev. Dr. Martin Luther King, Jr.

*We have to give our children, especially
Black boys, something to lose. Children make
foolish choices when they have nothing
to lose.*
—Dr. Jawanza Kunjufu

*He who starts behind in the great race of life must for-
ever remain behind or run faster than the man in front.*
—Dr. Benjamin E. Mays

*Children in families that eat dinner together
most nights each week are significantly less likely
to use illegal drugs, smoke, or abuse alcohol.*
—The National Center of Addiction and Substance
Abuse at Columbia University

*Lots of people limit their possibilities by giving up easily.
Never tell yourself this is too much for me. It's no use.*

I can't go on. If you do you're licked, and by your own thinking too. Keep believing and keep on keeping on.
—Dr. Norman Vincent Peale

Choice plus consequences equals responsibility.
— Dr. Michael H. Popkin

Poor self-esteem develops from receiving little or no feedback, being repeatedly criticized, receiving physical or mental abuse, feeling invisible, or feeling unloved.
—Popov, *The Family Virtues Guide*

The pimps' jobs have become much easier because somebody's already groomed these children for this life. Seventy to 90 percent of these girls have already been abused in what is supposed to be the safety of their homes.
—Dalia Racine, DeKalb County Assistant District Attorney, GA

Africans came to America, BEFORE, DURING AND AFTER enslavement. Don't start our history at the end; start it at the beginning.
—Dr. Runoko Rashidi

History is a light that illuminates the past and a key that unlocks the door to the future.
—Dr. Runoko Rashidi

What you do for yourself, in large measure, depends on what you think of yourself. So if you think that

*you have no worthy history, that you come from noth-
ing, you will tend to act that out. But, if you think that
you come from greatness, you will aim for the stars.*
—Dr. Runoko Rashidi

*We realize that our future lies chiefly in our own
hands. We know that neither institution nor friends
can make a race stand unless it has strength in its
own foundation; that races like individuals must
stand or fall by their own merit; that to fully succeed they must practice the virtues of self-reliance,
self-respect, industry, perseverance, and economy.*
—Paul Robeson

Only a man's character is the real criterion of worth.
—Eleanor Roosevelt

When you cease to make a contribution, you begin to die.
—Eleanor Roosevelt

African History is simply the missing pages of world history.
—Arthur Schomburg

*[Hollywood has made] tarts of the Negro's daugh-
ters, crap shooters of his sons, obsequious Uncle Toms
of his fathers, superstitious and grotesque crones
of his mothers, strutting peacocks of his successful men, psalm-singing mountebanks of his priests,
and Barnum and Bailey side-shows of his religion.*
—Dalton Trumbo, screenwriter

Every great dream begins with a dreamer. Always remember you have within you the strength, patience, and passion to reach for the stars to change the world.
—Harriet Tubman

Nutrition is vital for brain growth in the first three years of life…and lack of food can stunt the size and wiring of kids' brains. Poorly nourished children can have delays in development that affect IQ. While experts say most hungry Americans will not starve to death, people who don't have enough food, and enough of the right food, will not thrive—a condition called food insecurity.
—Dr. Renee M. Turchi

Unity is the fuel that allows common people to attain uncommon results.
—Unknown

I have begun everything with the idea that I could succeed and I never had much patience with the multitudes of people who are always ready to explain why one cannot succeed.
—Booker T. Washington

The individual who can do something that the world wants done will, in the end, make his way regardless of his race.
—Booker T. Washington

Black Children are our most valuable possession and our greatest potential resource. Any meaningful discussion of the survival or the future of Black people must be

*predicated upon Black people's plan for maximal develop-
ment of all Black children. Children are the only future
of any people. If children's lives are squandered, and if the
children of a people are not fully developed at whatever
cost and sacrifice, the people will have cosigned themselves
to certain death. They will be destroyed from without
and from within—by the attack of their own children
against them. And they may be destroyed by both.*
—Dr. Frances Cress Welsing

*What must we as Black women do? It is my convic-
tion that the African proverb 'the hand that rocks the
cradle rules the nation and its destiny' is true. Black
women are the mothers and, thus, the first teachers of
Black females and Black males alike. With increased
consciousness of their importance as the first teachers,
Black women can determine whether future generations
of Black children will be warriors or if we will continue
to be slaves living in a highly refined state of psychological oppression, which is no less a death than direct physical destruction. Black women as mothers and teachers can
teach the first powerful lessons in pride and respect for
cultural, historical and genetic Blackness, while stead-
fastly refusing to impart any part of the white oppressors'
lesson in Black self-hate that we learn as children...*
—Dr. Frances Cress Welsing, *The Isis Papers*

*We Black people do not see the war being waged against
us because we don't want to and because we are afraid.
We are engaging in behavior designed specifically to block*

out any awareness of the war -- our true reality. Our behavior thus forces us into the insanity of hoping and begging -- as opposed to the sanity of analysis, specific behavioral pattern design and specific conduct in all areas of people activity...Because we do not understand what is going on, in our impotence and ignorance, in our powerlessness and frustration, we start getting mad, fussing, crying, rhyming, begging with picket signs, rioting in misdirection, whooping and hollering, moaning in our churches and preparing to vote for any white man who smiles at us even though he lies to us. These behaviors are absolutely useless. Such behaviors are in vain and will take us nowhere. They will all come to naught and the problem—the war—will simply continue and intensify.
—Dr. Frances Cress Welsing, *The Isis Papers*

The mere imparting of information is not education. Above all things, the effort must result in making a man think and do for himself.
—Dr. Carter G. Woodson

When you control a man's thinking, you do not have to worry about his actions. You do not have to tell him not to stand here or go yonder. He will find his "proper place" and will stay in it. You do not need to send him to the back door. He will go without being told. In fact, if there is no back door, he will cut one for his special benefit. His education makes it necessary.
—Dr. Carter G. Woodson

Some children who have been sexually abused equate love with sex and abuse because their boundaries have been violated. There are feelings of guilt and shame instead of a thriving self-worth. Add the likelihood of poverty, and by the time these girls are approached by a trafficker, many are desperate not only for someone who can provide food, clothing and shelter but also affection.

—YouthSpark, Inc. Reports

Testimonials

When you actively love your children, your children will actively love and honor you back. In addition to the touching and sentimental words in a card, here are some handwritten notes added to the card from our children to us. This makes our parenting efforts so worth it! These are the crying-for-happy moments!

"Thank you for correcting my grammar at the dinner table. Thank you for not letting me sleep out. Thank you for waiting up and worrying about me. Thank you for taking me and my friends to the art museum. Thank you for accepting that I want to be an actor. Thank you for making me who I am today. I love you, Mother."

"In church they told us that we should thank the people that have helped you get where you are. I decided to send you a present and tell you thank you for all you have done for me. Mom, thank you for reading to me when I was little, feeding me vegetables, taking me to church, editing all of my papers, taking me to museums, nagging me about Goldenseal, coming to my track meets, buying me gold even though I always lost it, my 16th surprise birthday party, keeping important secrets, listening to my problems, teaching me about African-American history and so many more things. Dad, Thank you for teaching me how to play baseball, taking me to school when I was late, letting me go to Mexico, driving long hours to bring me home from school, turning off the TV when I forgot, the memories of eating eggs, bacon & grits at 6:00 in the morning, not getting as mad as you want to, cooking great pancakes, & letting Michael and I build houses in the backyard. These are just some things that stick out in my mind. Well, I have a lot of work to do so I gotta go. I hope the shirts fit. Dad, let me know if yours is too small. Love,"

"Mom, Hope you can find something nice with the money I sent."

"Thank you, Mom for standing by me through the good times as well as the bad. Love you always,"

"Thank you, Dad for everything. Love,"

"This was the perfect card! Thank you so much for coming down to take care of me like you always do. ☺ Love,"

"I'm so glad you're going to show the world how a true mother should be. Love always,"

"Dear Mom and Dad, I cannot express how grateful I am to have the both of you as parents. Everything you both have done has made me who I am today. The love you two have shown me to put out into the world is the greatest gift you have given me. Wish I could be home. Have a wonderful Christmas. Love,"

"Mom, you have always been there for me when I needed you. You have taught me love, and I am so grateful to have you as my mother. Love,"

"I'm truly grateful for all of your love. Love,"

"Thank you for making me the man I am today. You are wonderful parents and I am very blessed. Love,"

"Mom, thank you for making me the compassionate person I am today. Love,"

"Thank you for all of the love and support. I hope you have a wonderful birthday. Wish we could be there! Love,"

"Mom, I cannot express how grateful I am that you are my mother. You have impacted me tremendously throughout my life. Thank you so much for always being there for me. You are the perfect mother. Love,"

"Dad, I thank God that I am lucky enough to have you and mom as my parents. You make me into the strong person I am today. Love,"

"Mom & Dad, I wish I could be with you guys for Christmas, but I hope you enjoy your present. :) You really needed it!! I will see you before New Years!! Love,"

"Thank you, Mom for being the perfect mother to me. I have truly been blessed. Love,"

"I hope you have a wonderful birthday. I thought you would like to go shopping. Enjoy☺ Love,"

"Thank you, Mom for shaping me into the intelligent, compassionate and strong-willed man I am today. Both you and Dad have been perfect parents. Even though I may have made a few mistakes in life, I wouldn't change the way I am today. Thank you so much for always being there for me. You and Dad are a blessing to this world. Love,"

"lol…I thought you would laugh at this. Happy father's day! I have something for you and mom, but it will be there in 6-8 weeks! Love you!"

"Dad, Every time we ask you to go out, you prefer to stay at home and watch TV. This card has your 2 favorite places in the house. I guess you can add the kitchen also. Love you and thanks for always being there!"

"Great to celebrate your birthday with you. Love,"

"I love you granddad."

"Happy Grandma's day. Thank you. Love,"

"Thank you for participating in our wedding weekend. It was such a pleasure to have you share this special day with us. We hope that you enjoyed yourselves. We will send some formal photos when they are developed. Thank you for your generous gifts. We are going to use it toward our honeymoon in April. We hope to see you again soon. Love,"

"We had so much fun over the holidays. We are glad that we were able to be together. Thank you for the gifts. Love,"

"Thank you for hosting us for Christmas dinner and for the beautiful earrings. It's nice to spend the holidays with family. Tell April to give me a call when she gets to DC. Happy New Year."

"Hope you're on the golf course for your birthday. This is just in case you don't hit a hole-in-one. ☺"

"Dad, Thank you for being such a great father. Without you I wouldn't be the man I am today. Love,"

"I hope you have a wonderful day! I wish I could be there."

"Mom, I know your book will do very well. Every other mother has a lot to learn from you. Love,"

"Thank you so much for your help, Debby! We hope that you enjoy the book! Love,"

"Dad, Thank you for always being there. Knowing that you believe in me gave me the confidence to travel the world and know that I could do anything I put my mind to. Thank you for giving me the platform I needed to be successful in life. You and mom did a great job!"

"Dad, I just wanted to tell you. I love you. Happy Father's Day,"

"Dad, You have always been an amazing father. It is always an honor to hear people say I am just like you. Love you, Dad."

"Mom & Dad, I can't express how much I love you both. You have always been amazing parents and I am truly grateful to have you both. Love,"

"Mom, Keep pushing to finish the book. I have a great feeling about it. You are an amazing person. Love,"

A Parent's Pledge

I, as a parent, promise to give my child unconditional love.

I promise to make my child feel validated, seen, and heard.

I promise to separate my child's worth from their accomplishments and mistaken actions.

I promise to teach my child positive values and ethics.

I promise to meet with my child's teachers at school and take an active partnership in school education.

I promise to show appreciation to my child's uniqueness and efforts.

I promise to teach my child the proud history of our people and to let no one defile that history.

I promise to practice active listening everyday with my child.

I promise to teach my child to walk with truth, honesty, integrity, and forthrightness and model this behavior myself.

I promise to teach my child to love and respect themselves and others.

I promise to teach my child to do unto others as they would have others do unto them.

I promise to plan and participate in an activity with my child on a regular basis

I promise not to carry over yesterday's conflicts and disappointments into the next day. Each day will start fresh and positive.

I promise to teach my child there is no free lunch and to not feel entitled to anything for which they have not worked and struggled.

I promise to teach my child not to accept injustice from anyone.

I promise to teach my child that designer clothing is insignificant to personal development and accomplishments of goals and dreams.

I promise to teach my child that one's measure of worth is found in one's character, mind, and heart and not found in what one is wearing.

By Deborah Kelly

A Child's Pledge

I promise to love myself and all others (love begins within me and spreads outward).

I promise to reject hate and to turn away from feelings of non brotherhood.

I promise to reject anything that leads to self-destruction like drugs and alcohol, which is a form of slavery.

I promise to build my self-worth with my character and not with designer labels

I promise to send positive messages to myself, such as "I am a great person and I like me."

I promise to forgive those who have hurt me; carrying a grudge can lead to self-destruction and is not beneficial for me.

I promise to give and help those who are less fortunate. Blessings are received through giving; it is better to give than receive.

I promise to express my frustrations verbally and not physically. Self-preservation is a goal.

I promise to treat others as I would want to be treated.

I promise to show respect to myself and others.

I promise to let no one violate me. I teach people how to treat me, and I love and value myself.

I promise not to steal or take what does not belong to me.

I promise to give a kind word to another person within a day. I have the power to make my day better and someone else's day better.

I promise to be happy for the success of others, and I will be humble with my success. True worth is found in one's character.

I promise to use honesty and integrity and to tell the truth.

I promise to show mercy and understanding to others.

I promise to be a change agent for good, creating a positive environment, which begins with me.

By Deborah Kelly

A Child's Chant

I will be kind with a kind word for all.
I am kind.

I will be my own best friend.
I am a great person.

I will strive for excellence in school.
Education is a key to success.
I am intelligent.

I will be happy for the success of others.
I am encouraging.

I will not steal or tell the untruth.
I am honest.

I will not physically or verbally hurt anyone and will not allow anyone to hurt me.
I am peaceful.

I will feel hurt when others are hurting.
I am compassionate.

I will turn away from drugs and alcohol. Addiction is a form of slavery.
I like myself.

I will forgive others as I would want to be for-
given. Forgiving frees us from self-hurt.
I am strong.

When I am hurt, I will express myself
verbally and not physically.
I am valuable.

I will treat others the way I want to be treated.
I am considerate.

I will give to others and build up my community.
I am capable.

I will turn away from hate and
keep love in my heart.
I am love.

By Deborah Kelly

Teach Me

By RuNett Nia Ebo

Teach me all the things you think I need to know.

Tell me of the places where you believe I ought to go.

Show me where you've been and
what I need to do to get there.

Describe the schools where you learned and
the people that you met there.

Guide me in finding the truth in life because
I'll never respect a lie.

Give me answers to my questions, especially when I ask "Why?".

Help me not to make mistakes but when I do,
please be forgiving.

Teach me **how to live**—<u>not just</u> how to make a living!

Children Learn What They Live

By Dorothy Law Nolte

If a child lives with criticism, he learns to condemn.

If a child lives with hostility, he learns to fight.

If a child lives with ridicule, he learns to be shy.

If a child lives with shame, he learns to feel guilty.

If a child lives with tolerance, he learns to be patient.

If a child lives with encouragement, he learns confidence.

If a child lives with praise, he learns to appreciate.

If a child lives with fairness, he learns justice.

If a child lives with security, he learns to have faith.

If a child lives with approval, he learns to like himself.

If a child lives with acceptance and friendship,
he learns to find love in the world

Today

By Deborah Bussey Staton Kelly

Yesterday, I dreamed of happiness. I waited for it
to happen like daybreak cracking into darkness.
I wondered why life was so cruel and unoblig-
ing, reacting to good times and crying when bad.
Yesterday, I searched my soul for the "whys"
and "why nots." Today, I act and reach out.

Parent Reading Guide

Multicultural Parenting Resources

Abboud, Soo Kim and Jane Kim. 2005. *Top of the Class: How Asian Parents Raise High Achievers and How You Can Too*. New York: Penguin Publishing Group.

Akua, Chike. *Parent Power!: The Keys to Your Child's Academic and Social Success*.

Armstrong, Thomas. 1999. *7 Kinds of Smart*. New York: Plume.

Clark, Jean Illsley and Connie Dawson. 1998. *Growing Up Again*. Center City: Hazelden.

Coloroso, Barbara. 1995. *Kids Are Worth It! Giving Your Child the Gift of Inner Discipline*. New York: Avon Books.

Corkille Briggs, Dorothy. 1970. *Your Child's Self-Esteem, Step-by-Step Guidelines for Raising Responsible, Productive, Happy Children*. New York: Doubleday Dell.

Doman, Glenn. 1982. *How to Teach Your Baby to Read*. New York: Random House.

Doman, Glenn. 1982. *Teach Your Baby Math*. Pocket Books, New York: Simon & Schuster.

Eyre, Richard and Linda. 1984. *Teaching Your Children Responsibility*. New York: Fireside Book.

Faber, Adele and Elaine Mazlish. 1999. *How To Talk So Kids Will Listen & Listen So Kids Will Talk*. New York: Avon Books.

Faber, Adele and Elaine Mazlish. 1990. *Liberated Parents, Liberated Children Your Guide To A Happier Family*. New York: Avon Books.

Kunjufu, Dr. Jawanza. 2000. *Developing Positive Self-Images & Discipline in Black Children*. Chicago: African-American Images.

McGoldrick, Monica. 1995. *You Can Go Home Again, Reconnecting with Your Family*. New York: W. W. Norton & Co., Inc.

Pipher, Mary. 1997. *The Shelter of Each Other Rebuilding Our Families*. New York: Ballantine Books.

Popkin, Dr. Michael H. 1983. *Active Parenting Hand Book*. Atlanta: Active Parenting.

Popov, Linda Kavelin, Dan Popov, and John Kavelin. 1997. *The Family Virtues Guide, Simple Ways to Bring Out the Best in Our Children and Ourselves*. New York: Plume Book.

Rodriguez, Gloria. 1999. *Raising Nuestros Ninos: Bringing Up Latino Children in a Bicultural World*. New York: Fireside.

Wagenhals, Diane. 2005. *PREN's Parents Reference Guide: 25 Essential Tools and Tips You Need for Emotionally Healthy Parenting*. Fort Washington: PREN.

The New American Webster Dictionary.

Ethnic Book Resources

Addae, Erriel Kofi. 1996. *To Heal a People: African Scholars Defining a New Reality*. Columbia: Kujichagulia Press.

Akbar, Na'im. 1994. *Light From Ancient Africa*. Tallahassee: Mind Productions.

Akua, Chike. *Honoring Our Ancestral Obligations: 7 Steps to Black Student Success*.

Alexander, Michelle. 2010. *The New Jim Crow, Mass Incarceration in the Age of Colorblindness*. New York: The New Press.

Bell, Janet Cheatham. 1986. *Famous Black Quotations and Some Not So Famous*. Chicago: Famous Black Quotations.

Bell, Janet Cheatham. 1991. *Famous Black Quotations, On Women, Love, and Other Topics*. Chicago: Famous Black Quotations.

Ben-Jochannan, Dr. Yosef A. A. 1989. *Black Man of the Nile and His Family*. Baltimore: Black Classic Press.

Bennett, Lerone, Jr. 1988. *Before The Mayflower, A History of Black America*. New York: Penguin Books, Johnson Publishing Co.

Billingsley, Andrew. 1992. *Climbing Jacob's Ladder: The Enduring Legacy of African-American Families*. New York: Simon and Schuster.

Browder, Anthony T. 1992. *Nile Valley Contributions to Civilization*. Washington: The Institute of Karmic Guidance.

Browder, Anthony T. 1996. *Survival Strategies for Africans in America*. Washington: The Institute of Karmic Guidance.

Brown, Tony. 1995. *Black Lies, White Lies, The Truth According to Tony Brown*. New York: William Morrow and Company, Inc.

Diop, Dr. Cheikh Anta. 1987. *Precolonial Black Africa*. Brooklyn: Lawrence Hill Books.

Douglass, Frederick. 1892. *The Most Complete Collection of Written Works & Speeches*. Northpointe Classics.

Dubois, Dr. W.E.B. 2012. *The Souls of Black Folk*. Dover Publications, unabridged.

Fanon, Frantz. 1963. *The Wretched of the Earth*. New York: Grove Press, Inc.

Feagin, Joe R. and Melvin P. Sikes. *Living With Racism: The Middle Class Experience*.

Freire, Paulo. 2000. *Pedagogy of the Oppressed*. New York: Continuum Books, The Seabury Press.

Franklin, John Hope. 1969. *From Slavery to Freedom: A History of Negro Americans, 3rd Edition*. New York: Vintage Books, Random House.

Higginbotham, A. Leon, Jr. 1978. *In the Matter of Color, Race & The American Legal Process: The Colonial Period*. New York: Oxford University Press.

Hilliard, Asa. 1997. *The Reawakening of the African Mind*. Gainesville: Makare Publishing Co.

James, George. 1954. *Stolen Legacy*. Newport: United Brothers Communication Systems.

Kunjufu, Dr. Jawanza. 1982. *Countering the Conspiracy to Destroy Black Boys, Revised Edition*. Chicago: African-American Images.

Locke, Alain. 1925. *The New Negro Voices of the Harlem Renaissance*. New York: Touchstone.

Osaze, Jabari. 2016. *Seven Little White Lies: The Conspiracy to Destroy the Black Self Image*. Philadelphia: African Genesis Institute Press.

Rashidi, Dr. Runoko and Ivan Van Sertima. 1988. *African Presence in Early Asia*. New Brunswick: Transaction Publishers.

Rashidi, Dr. Runoko. 2011. *Black Star, The African Presence in Early Europe*. London: Books of Africa, Ltd.

Reclamation Project. 2014. *How White Folks Got So Rich, The Untold Story of American White Supremacy*. The Reclamation Project.

Robinson, Clavin R., Redman Battle, and Dr. Edward W. Robinson, Jr. 1987. *The Journey of the Songhai People, 2nd Edition*. Philadelphia: The Pan African Federation Organization.

Rogers, J. A. and Helga Rogers. 1995. *100 Amazing Facts About the Negro*. St. Petersburg: Wesleyan University Press.

Sertima, Ivan Van. 1991. *Golden Age of the Moor*. Transaction Publisher.

Sertima, Ivan Van. 2003. *They Came Before Columbus, The African Presence in Ancient America*. New York: Random House Trade.

Solow, Barbara L. 1991. *Slavery and the Rise of the Atlantic System*. Cambridge: Cambridge United Press.

Tait, Lewis T. and Christian Van Gorder. 2002. *Three-Fifths Theology: Challenging Racism in America*. Trenton: Africa World Press.

Washington, Booker T. 2010. *Up From Slavery: An Autobiography*. Dover Publications.

Welsing, Dr. Frances Cress. 1991. *The Isis Papers*. Chicago: Third World Press.

Wise, Tim. 2010. *Color-Blind, The Rise of Post-Racial Politics and the Retreat from Racial Equity*. San Francisco: City Lights Books.

Woodson, Dr. Carter G. 2012. *Miseducation of the Negro*. Popular Classics Publishing.

GLOSSARY/DEFINITIONS

Abstain—Refrain from action

Accordance—Agreement or harmony

Acronyms—A word made from the initial letters of a term or phase (e.g., NAACP—National Association for the Advancement of Colored People)

Acrostics—Composition in which the initial letters or lines form a word or phrase (e.g., LOVE—Living with you has been joy, Only leaving would cause pain, Value every day with our love, Even to the end of our time will I love you)

Adjective—Part of speech that describes a noun and pronoun (e.g., great, brown, large, small)

Adverb—Part of speech that describes a verb, adjective, and other adverbs (e.g., greatly, slowly, swiftly, really, quickly)

Affirmation—Declare and confirm as positive

Aggregate—Collect into a sum, mass, or body

Analogy—Comparison of two things similar in nature but different (e.g., the heart of a body is as an engine of a car)

Anecdote—A short story of an occurrence

Anesthetize—Loss or deadening of feelings

Antibodies—An immunization that counteracts malignant bacteria in the body

Articulate—Say or speak distinctly

Assemble—Bring together in one piece, fit together

Asset—Anything owned of value

Attribute—Characteristic

Auditory—Pertaining to the sense of hearing

Autonomy—Self-governing, independent

Bad touch—A touch that makes one feel uncomfortable or uneasy

Balloon rate—When the installment payments on a loan goes up at a designated time

Benchmark—A point of reference for making measurements

Benefactor—Recipient of a benefit

Bilingual—Able to speak two languages

Biological lineage—Paternal (father) or maternal (mother) biological/genetic ancestry

Black—Operating in the "black" is when a company is operating at a profit

Bottom line—Profit margin

By-product—An additional result or effect of intended action

Capital—Money, buildings, machinery, tools, anything of value owned

Capital Resources—Money, buildings, machinery, tools used in producing goods and services.

Catapult—A launching from which to go upward

Cognitive—Conscious awareness development

Coincide—To concur or agree

Collateral—Something given (personal property) as additional security for a loan

Commensurate—Comparable in amount, degree, and size

Commodity—A useful thing that can be traded

Compassion—Sympathy, pity

Compatible—Consistent or agreeable with

Competency—A task or skill

Compromise—The settlement of differences by mutual concession

Comradeship—Act of being close friends

Concept—An idea or thought

Conducive—Contribute to a result

Conjugation of verbs—Inflection of verbs (e.g., run, ran, have/had run; come, came, have/had come; go, went, have/had gone)

Consequence—That which follows as a result or after some action

Constructive Feedback—Giving suggestions to improve behavior

Contextual learning—Learning that is done when learners are able to base learning on their experiences

Copyright—The exclusive right to use or reproduce a literary or artistic work

Core belief system—Center of who we believe we are by way of outward messages

Correlate—Related or connected

Cosign—When someone else agrees to pay if the original borrower defaults (doesn't pay)

Credit—Borrowing power, payment received, acknowledgment of worth

Credit card—Borrowing money from an issuer (bank or credit union) with the promise to pay it back at an interest rate

Criteria—Standard for comparison or judgment

Culmination—Result of reaching the highest point

Cultivate—Promote the growth of

Debit—Recorded item of payment made

Debit card—Using your own money held with an issuer (bank or credit union)

Decipher—Find meaning of, decode

Default—Fail to make payment

Delegate—Empower another person to act on your behalf

Demand—What buyers are willing to buy at a particular price

Derive—Receive from a source

Deteriorate—Reduce in worth

Detriment—That which causes injury or loss

Dialogue—Conversation between two or more people

Diminish—Make less or smaller

Discretionary income—Money earned that is used at your discretion for pleasure, comfort, entertainment, and non-survival expenditures (e.g., theater, movie, restaurants, sports events, and designer items, etc.)

Disintegrate—Separate into parts, go to pieces

Disposable income—Money earned that is used for survival expenditures (e.g., food, clothing, shelter—rent or mortgage)

Disposition—Natural temperament of the mind

Dracula Syndrome—When victims make others their victims

Dysfunctional—Not useful for working toward the good

Economic Resources—Capital, Natural, and Human Resources used in the production of goods and services

Economical—How money and expenditures are made, spent, and produced

Element—Component

Empathy—Sympathetic understanding of another's feelings or situation

Empower—Authorize or give power

Emulate—Strive to be equal to, imitate

Engage—Gain the attention of

Enunciate—Pronounce distinctively

Environment—Totality of external influences (e.g., home, school, church, synagogue, mosque, relatives, friends)

Equity—Net financial interest in a property

Exalt—Praise or honor

Extracurricular activities—Offered in addition to basic or standard school curriculum (e.g., sports, music, clubs, and enrichment activities)

Facilitate—Make easier

Fallacy—A false idea or perception

Feces—Excrement, defecation, bowel movement

Federal Deposit Insurance Corporation (FDIC)—Federal agency that protects depositors' money in case of failure of a bank or financial institution that it regulates

Fervor—Intensity of feeling or expression

Fluctuate—Rise and fall

Formative—Formation or development at a young age

Foundational skills—Basic skills on which other skills are built (e.g., reading, writing, math)

Genetically Modified Organism—When the heredity or evolution of a gene is altered

Good touch—Touches that feel comfortable and safe

Gratitude—Thankfulness

Haggle—Dispute and bargain for lower price

Heredity—The transmission of qualities or characteristics from parent gene to offspring

Heterogeneous grouping—Composed of different kinds (e.g., male and female combined grouping)

Homogeneous grouping—Composed of the same kind (e.g., all-male or all-female grouping)

Human Resources—People who work for a business who have knowledge, skill, expertise, integrity, honesty, are on time, are decision makers, and are problem solvers.

Humility—To show gratitude without being cocky or arrogant

Ideology—Aggregate of beliefs, ideas, and doctrines

Idiom—Phrase which you look at whole for meaning (e.g., having two left feet, having a green thumb, raining cats and dogs)

Immune System—System in the human body capable of fighting diseases

Impede—To hinder or obstruct the progress of

Imperishable—Not easily spoiled

Increment—Something added or increased

Infrastructure—The fundamental facilities and systems serving a county, country, or area including communications, transportation, power plants, sanitation, educational systems

Input—The energy or power put into something

Installments—A method of payment by dividing total into individual payments

Insolvent—Having greater liabilities than assets

Intangible—Not being able to touch, smell, and see

Inaction—Action between or among each other

Internalize—Taken into self and used

Intrinsic—Being an innate or essential part of

IRA (individual retirement account)—Savings account with the government for retirement, including 403B (government entities), 401K (privately owned companies), and independent accounts

Investment—Return on profitable use of money/other asset

Jaundiced eye—A feeling of distrust that colors judgment

Latter—Being the second of two mentioned

Lender—Entity (bank, credit union, family member or friend) who gives temporary custody of money or other valuables, creditor

Liability—Things owed against assets

Lifelong learning—A need to learn during one's entire life

Lifestyle—A person's specific way of living

Liquidity—Easily converted to cash with little consequences

Literal—True to facts or interpretation

Logo—Company symbol (e.g., Nike swoosh)

Manifest—Evidenced in outward behavior

Marginal—On the edge or limited in scope

Merchant—One who buys and sells commodities

Mind's Eye—What you see in your mind becomes a visualization

Mnemonics—Memorization techniques (e.g., repetition, association, using senses)

Money opportunities—Ways of acquiring assets such as money or bartering

Monolingual—Able to speak one language

Mores—Customs of behavior

Natural Resources—Raw materials that come from the land, water, and air (e.g., produce, oil, diamonds, gems, gold, silver, valuable chemicals, fish, fowl)

Negotiation—To bring about mutual settlement

Neurons—Nerve cells that connect to behaviors

Neutralize—To counteract or become inactive

Noun—Part of speech that is a person, place, thing, or thought (e.g., home, city, state, country, continent, sincerity, loyalty)

Objective—Goal or aim

Obesity—Being very fat

Paralyze—Render ineffective

Paraphrase—The same meaning in other words

Patent—Temporary exclusive use of an invention

Pedagogy—Teaching skills, procedures, and techniques

Phonetics—In spelling, always using the same symbol for each same sound

Posit—Present as a fact

Precede—Something that comes before

Precedence—The right of taking a more honored position

Precedent—Identical previous example

Prerequisite—Something needed in advance

Processed foods—Foods that are processed/changed from one form to another

Profound—Intense, deeply felt

Proactive—Plan and act toward a desired outcome

Proficiency—Skilled or expert level

Profit—Excess of return over cost

Promiscuity—Indiscriminate sexual relations

Pronoun—Part of speech that takes the place of a noun (e.g., it, he, she, you, them, they)

Provocative—Stimulate or arouse

Public Goods—Goods and services provided to a community by the government through tax payments including schools, parks, civic centers (where plays and concerts are performed), trash collection, street/road and bridge repair

Quotient—The number produced by dividing a given number by another

Recall skills—Act of remembering

Reciprocal (Reciprocity)—A mutually give and return relationship

Red—Operating in the "red" is when a company is operating at a loss

Regimentation—Act of bringing under uniform control

Reinforcement—Strengthening or support of

Relevant—Applicable and concerning the case in question

Repentance—Showing regret or grief

Restitution—The act of returning or restoring what was lost

Restoration—The act of bringing back to original state

Retail—Sale of goods to consumers

Retention—Act of retaining memory

Sabotage—To willfully and maliciously destroy or impede

Scenario—Developing an outline of a story or scene

Self-actualized—Result of developmental needs being met toward self-fulfillment

Self-esteem—How one feels about oneself, self-image of worth

Self-concept—How one feels others feel about self

Self-fulfilling prophecy—Anticipation and belief in outcome will put behavior in place to make that outcome happen

Self-sabotage—Nonproductive behavior that impedes our own success

Self-validation—To approve and emotionally support oneself

Self-worth—Giving oneself value and merit

Sibling—A brother or sister

Simultaneous—Existing or operating at the same time

Skill-set—A group of skill/knowledge expertise

Solvent—Able to pay all debts

Spontaneity—Natural, impulsive actions

Spouse—One's husband or wife

Stereotype—Prejudgment of image or actions assigned to people

Success mind-set—Determination to be prosperous and accomplished

Suffice—Being enough, being adequate

Supersede—Replace, set aside

Supply—What and how much sellers are willing to sell

Surrogate—A substitute

Sweat equity—Amount of physical and mental work

Tactile—Pertaining to the sense of touch

Tangible—Capable of being touched, seen, and heard and capable of being realized

Temperament—Natural personality disposition

Tenet—Any principle, opinion, or doctrine held to be true

Terrible Twos—When a child feels more secure as an independent person and begins to act defiant

Trademark—Registered company symbol or logo

Transfer Skills—Skills/knowledge learned in one setting that can be used in another setting

Ubiquitous—Being everywhere at the same time

Unconditional love—Total acceptance and love regardless of circumstances

Unsavory—Disagreeable, not beneficial to self or lifestyle

Usurp—Seize or hold without right

Uterus—The female organ in which the fetus rest and grows, the womb

Validate—To make important, secure, or sound

Veracity—Truthfulness

Verb—Part of speech that is an action word (e.g. run, sit, eat, is, are, be, been, were)

Violate—Break or infringe upon

Visualization—Form a mental image of what is desired

Vocational School—Schools that specialize in trade and skill education

Volume—Quantity

Vulnerable—Susceptible to being wounded or damaged

Wholesale—Sale of goods in quantity to retailers

Window of opportunity—An opening when skills can be developed at its maximum

Index

Made in the USA
Monee, IL
28 October 2022

16753731R00132